THE AMAZING BOOK OF
PAPER BOATS

THE AMAZING BOOK OF
PAPER BOATS

Created and Produced by Melcher Media

Illustrations and Paper Engineering by Willy Bullock

Research and Narrative Text by Jerry Roberts

chronicle books · san francisco

This book was produced by Melcher Media, Inc.,
55 Vandam Street, New York, NY 10013,
under the editorial direction of Charles Melcher.

Editors: Gillian Sowell and Colin Dickerman
Design: Empire Design Studio, NYC
Production Director: Andrea Hirsh
Model Photographer: Dan Howell
Line Editor: Ellyn Hament
Printing through Asia Pacific Offset

Special thanks to Duncan Bock, David Bowers, Sharon Bowers, Molly Cooper, Jenni Gray, Anne Hartshorn,
the Intrepid Sea Air Space Museum, the Pastan clan, Victoria Rock, Jennifer Vetter, Lauren Weinberger,
and Megan Worman.

Grateful acknowledgment is made to the following people and institutions for permission to reproduce photographs:
Michael Cullen, The Canadian Canoe Museum (page 20); Alison Langley/Stock Newport (pages 32, 44, 71);
Dan LeMaire (page 66); courtesy of the Mariners' Museum, Newport News, Va. (pages 31, 48, 49, 60, 70, 75, 76);
Peter McGowan/Stock Newport (pages 23, 24, 43); photographer unknown/National Archives of Canada/PA-022366
(page 19); Sarah Shapiro/Stock Newport (page 65); Rick Tomlinson/Stock Newport (page 36); Rick Tomlinson
Photography/courtesy National Royal Lifeboat Institution (pages 39, 40); courtesy United States Naval Institute Photo
Archives (pages 35, 55, 56, 61); Onne van der Wal (pages 27, 28).

ISBN 0-8118-2939-1

Distributed in Canada by Raincoast Books
9050 Shaughnessy Street, Vancouver, British Columbia V6P 6E5

10 9 8 7 6 5 4 3 2 1

Chronicle Books LLC
85 Second Street, San Francisco, California 94105
www.chroniclebooks.com

CONTENTS

A BRIEF HISTORY OF BOATS	7	
HOW BOATS FLOAT	11	
ASSEMBLY TIPS & TECHNIQUES	15	
NAUTICAL TERMS	18	

	Descriptions and Assembly Instructions	The Models
◄ Bark Canoe (#1)	19	81
◄ Bark Canoe (#2)	19	81
◄ Rowboat (#1)	23	83
◄ Rowboat (#2)	23	85
◄ ◄ Offshore Racing Boat (#1)	27	87
◄ ◄ Offshore Racing Boat (#2)	27	89
◄ ◄ Mahogany Runabout	31	93
◄ ◄ Coast Guard Boat	35	95
◄ ◄ Rescue Lifeboat	39	97
◄ ◄ Sailboat (#1)	43	99
◄ ◄ Sailboat (#2)	43	103
◄ ◄ *Monitor*	48	107
◄ ◄ *Merrimack*	48	109
◄ ◄ Aircraft Carrier	55	113
◄ ◄ PT Boat	60	117
◄ ◄ ◄ Tugboat	65	119
◄ ◄ ◄ Ocean Liner	70	121
◄ ◄ ◄ Mississippi Paddle Wheeler	75	123

◄ Easy   ◄ ◄ Mid-level   ◄ ◄ ◄ Challenging

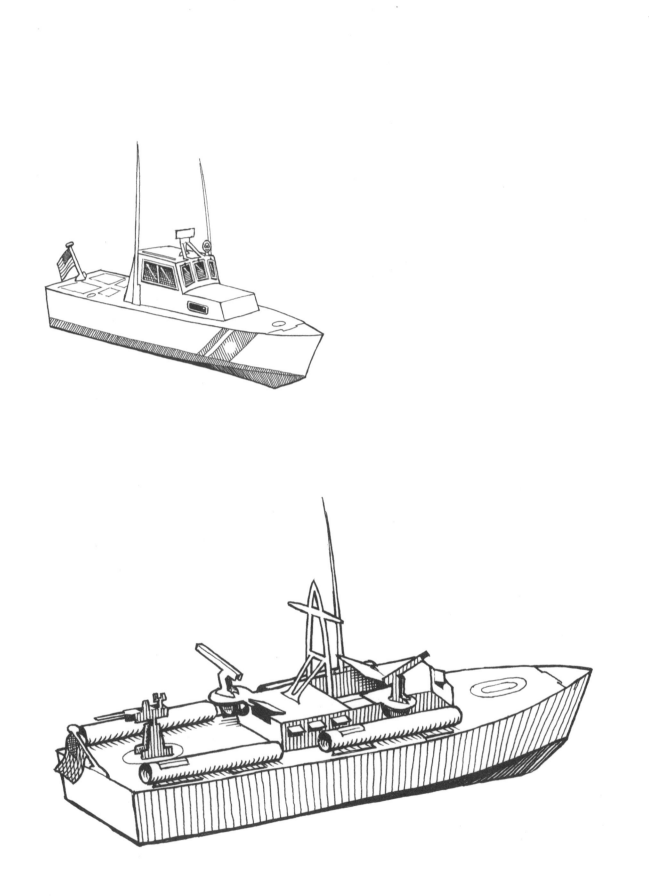

A BRIEF HISTORY OF BOATS

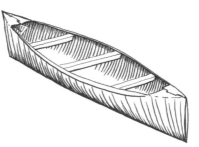

In the pages that follow, you'll learn the stories behind eighteen different boats—from small, sturdy rowboats and dinghies to huge, powerful ocean liners and aircraft carriers. You'll discover exactly how ships float, and how they've evolved. Using the models at the back of this book, which are printed on waterproof paper, you can also build and float paper versions of all the boats in this book— and create your own private fleet.

As you read about and build models of boats, consider this: You're part of a long tradition. Humans have been building boats for at least 30,000 years. All sorts of materials, from reeds and animal skins, to planks, steel, and fiberglass, are used to make real boats. There are special vessels for every job you can imagine. Some are work boats, such as tugboats and fishing trawlers. Some take us places, like ocean liners and ferries. Warships are built to defend us, rescue vessels offer help when there's trouble at sea, and deep-diving submersibles are for research and exploration. And some vessels, like rowboats, sailboats, canoes, kayaks, and motorboats, are built just for fun. While boats come in many shapes and sizes, and perform different functions, they share a common promise of adventure.

Your own adventure might begin with a tugboat in the backyard swimming pool, or a mahogany runabout in a nearby pond. Your vessel might be a Mississippi paddle wheeler in a local creek, or an aircraft carrier in the bathtub. Whatever watercraft you choose in this book, you'll be off on an exciting nautical journey.

WHEN IS A BOAT A SHIP?

Before looking back at the history of water travel, you may be wondering what the difference is between a "boat" and a "ship." An easy answer is that boats are small and ships are big, but that's not always true. Some tugboats are huge, and all submarines, even the largest in the world, are called boats. Sometimes, people claim that a ship can carry a boat but a boat can't carry a ship. That's correct, but a better explanation is that boats are usually used in coastal waters, within about fifty miles of land. Ships, however, are built to travel long distances in the open sea. Still, some boats are strong enough to face the ocean, and many small boats have sailed around the world.

WHO BUILT THE FIRST BOATS?

Have you ever wondered who built the first boats? It's hard to say when they were made, or who built them, but we know why they were needed: to catch fish, transport passengers and cargo, fight wars, and explore new horizons.

Our prehistoric ancestors probably found that they could cross rivers or lakes by holding onto logs and kicking with their feet. One day, perhaps, someone tried to avoid getting wet and sat on a log in the water. It probably took some trial and error to discover which size log supported this person's weight, or how to keep from rolling off. Although he or she didn't know it at the time, this early adventurer was experimenting with the basics of buoyancy and stability, which still shape the way we design and build boats today. The next step toward inventing boats probably came when people started tying logs together into floating platforms we now call rafts.

About ten thousand years ago in Northern Europe, people began to stretch animal skins over wooden frames to make small round boats called "coracles." In Egypt, reeds were bundled together to make raft boats. A major breakthrough came when people began to hollow out logs so they could sit in—not just on—them. Boats made this way are called dugout canoes. Dugouts were used all over the world, and some of the oldest were made around eight thousand years ago. Large dugout canoes could hold several people and even cargo.

Eventually, Native people of North America (as well as others around the world) developed lightweight canoes made of

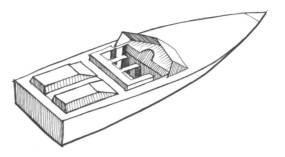

stitched tree bark reinforced with wooden ribs. Birch bark canoes were used for trading, hunting, fishing, and carrying supplies or warriors.

WHAT MADE THEM GO?

The first boats were all powered by human energy. People paddled with their hands or kicked with their legs. Poles were used to push logs and rafts along, but soon paddles were carved from wood, which allowed boats to venture into deeper water. Eventually oars, which are paddles that pivot on the side of a boat, were developed. But things really started moving when people discovered that they could harness the power of the wind in sails, which allowed them to travel greater distances at faster speeds. Although rafts remained stable even with a mast and a sail, dugout canoes needed the addition of outriggers (long poles connected to floats) to keep them from tipping over.

BOATS TO SHIPS

Boats began to grow larger when extra wooden planks were added to the sides of dugout canoes so they could carry more cargo through rougher water. As more and more planks were added, ribs were placed inside to help the vessel keep its shape. Once vessels became larger, and stable enough to travel on the open sea, they were no longer just boats—they had become ships.

By 3000 B.C., vessels known as "round ships" were carrying trade goods throughout the eastern Mediterranean. Their roomy hulls were suited to transporting cargo. "Long ships," also powered by sails and oars, were built expressly for fighting. Their leaner shape made them more maneuverable and faster. The Greeks and Romans expanded the use of both of these types of vessels. Their most famous warship was the trireme, a galley or long ship that carried hundreds of rowers on three levels.

In Scandinavia, the Vikings built large ships powered by both sails and oars. They also used round ships for trade, while their longboats were used for war and exploration. Many historians believe that Viking explorers were the first Europeans to reach North America in about A.D. 1000.

A major advance in shipbuilding began in Europe around A.D. 1300. Before that time, ships were made of wooden planks fastened to each other, with ribs and supports added inside for rigidity. Later, the keel and frame were built first and the planks fastened directly to them. With this system, larger and much stronger ships could be built. In fact, all wooden ships have been built this way ever since.

FROM SAILS TO STEAM

For thousands of years, sails powered boats and ships. Most early ships used a single

square sail or triangular sails on a single mast. But as technology evolved, ships were soon being built with several masts, each able to carry a number of sails. By the end of the 1400s, in the Age of Exploration, ships—like those sailed by Ferdinand Magellan and Christopher Columbus—had three masts with sophisticated sails and rigging.

The peak era of the wooden sailing ship was from the mid-1700s to the very beginning of the 1900s, when large powerful sailing ships were developed for both trade and battle. Some of the most beautiful and fastest sailing ships were called clipper ships. Eventually, some sailing ships could even cross the Atlantic from England to New York in fourteen days or less. But soon a more consistent power source was developed and the age of steam gradually replaced the age of sail.

Although the steam engine was invented in the late 1700s, the first practical steamships were not built until the early 1800s. In 1807, American inventor Robert Fulton successfully demonstrated his steamboat by making a run along the Hudson River between New York City and Albany, New York, in about one-quarter of the time it took a sailboat to make the same journey. Increasingly powerful steam engines soon powered larger and larger ships, including the great ocean liners of the early 20th century. Today many ships are powered by modern steam turbine engines, as well as powerful diesel engines, and even nuclear reactors.

FROM WOOD TO STEEL—AND BEYOND

As the technology that powered ships changed, so did the materials used to build them. After thousands of years of wooden construction, the first iron-hulled ships were built in the mid-1800s. Soon iron and steel became the standard material of large vessels around the world. Today, most ships are made of steel or aluminum.

Wood was still used for nearly all recreational boats until a new material called fiberglass revolutionized the small boat-building industry in the 1950s. Fiberglass is plastic resin reinforced with cloth made from strands of glass fiber. Unlike wood and steel, which has to be shaped and fastened to a frame, fiberglass boats can be mass-produced in molds, and fiberglass never rusts or rots. Today, small ships can be made this way. Perhaps someday even larger ships will be made of advanced composite materials.

The evolution of ships and boats from dugout canoes to giant ocean-going ships has helped shape our world through exploration, trade, transportation, and war. But this evolution is far from over. Every day faster, larger, and more efficient ships are being built to sail the oceans of the world.

HOW BOATS FLOAT

What makes a boat—or any object—float? Do things float because they are light and sink because they are heavy? Not really. A large ship, like an aircraft carrier, may weigh more than 80,000 tons, yet it floats very nicely. A fork, on the other hand, doesn't weigh much, perhaps a couple of ounces, but it won't float at all! They're both made of steel. So what really makes a boat float or sink?

According to legend, over 2,200 years ago Greek physicist Archimedes began to solve the mystery of how things float when he was taking a bath. He carelessly filled his bathtub to the very top and then got in. Naturally, the water overflowed. And that got him thinking.

DISPLACEMENT

Why does water overflow when you get into a full tub? The water overflows because your body takes up some of the room in the tub and two things cannot be in the same place at the same time. So your body pushes, or displaces, some of the water someplace else—probably onto the floor! This is called displacement.

The same thing will happen if you put a large toy boat in a sink. The boat will take up some of the room and it will displace some of the water. If you could scoop up all the water that the boat pushes out of the sink it will weigh the same as the boat. If the boat weighs ten pounds, it will push aside (displace) ten pounds of water in order to stay afloat. So we would say the boat has a displacement of ten pounds! It works the same way with real ships. But the ocean is so big that it will not overflow. The displaced water just moves aside.

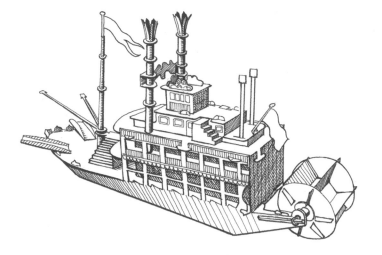

DENSITY

Some things are denser than others. A brick is denser than a sponge. Steel is denser than water. Water is denser than air. When something is very dense, that means it is packed tightly together. Sand is denser than corn flakes, and a candy bar is denser than cotton candy. If a boat is less dense than the water it displaces, it will float. If it is denser than the water, it will sink.

Steel is denser than water, but when it is in the form of a steel boat, it is not denser than water. A boat is not solid steel. It has space inside where there is no metal at all. There is lots of room in a ship for the crew to work and sleep, and for cargo to be stored. All of this space is filled with air, and air is much less dense than water. So even though steel is denser than water, if you add up all the steel and air inside the ship, the average is not as dense as the water around it.

Of course if the ship had a hole in it and filled with water, the water would replace the air inside and the ship would be more dense than the water around it. Then the ship would sink! What do you think would happen if you put too much cargo or too many people in a boat?

BUOYANCY

If you take an empty glass jar, screw the top on, and put it in the water, what will it do? It will float because the glass and air inside are not as dense as the water. When something floats we say it has positive buoyancy. If you now take the top off the jar and let it fill with water, what will happen? The jar will sink because without the air inside, the jar is denser than the water. When something sinks we say it has negative buoyancy.

If you fill the jar with just enough air and water so that it will float underwater without sinking, that is called neutral buoyancy. Submarines use special ballast tanks to switch between positive, neutral, and negative bouyancy in order to submerge and surface.

STABILITY

Now that you know how boats float, there's one more word you need to know before you go to sea: stability. Good stability is what keeps a boat from tipping over. If you sit in the bottom of a canoe with a bowling ball in your lap, you would have pretty good stability. Things have good stability when their center of gravity is low. For a boat, that means that the heaviest stuff is down low in the boat, rather than high up. But if you were to sit on one edge of the canoe and hold the bowling ball in your lap, the canoe would probably tip over, especially if a wave rocked the boat. This is because your center of gravity is too high, and your weight is not centered in the boat. You would have bad stability. It's the same with a ship. If you put all the cargo low in a ship, it will be stable. But if you put it all high up on the deck, or off to one side, the ship could tip over. Because sailboats and tall ships have tall masts, extra weight must be added to the bottom of the boat to keep the center of gravity low. Extra weight that is added to a boat is called ballast.

PROVE IT!

You can experiment with buoyancy, displacement, density, and stability right in your own sink or tub. You'll need an empty plastic gallon milk jug, a marker, a piece of aluminum foil about 5 inches square, and some marbles or small pebbles. First, make a simple displacement tank by cutting the top off the milk jug and filling it halfway with water. Use the marker to draw a line at the water level. Then bend the piece of foil into a dish-shaped boat and float it in your displacement tank. Now see how many marbles or pebbles you can put in it. As you put more weights into the boat, notice how the water line rises above the mark you made on the milk jug. This shows you how much water your boat displaces. You will find that if you put too many marbles on one side, your boat will become unstable and tip over. As long as your boat and its cargo are less dense than the water it displaces, it will have positive buoyancy and float. If you keep adding marbles, your boat will eventually sink when it reaches negative buoyancy.

When you build your paper boats, the instructions will tell you how to add some weight (ballast) to the bottom of the hulls to make them more stable.

ASSEMBLY TIPS & TECHNIQUES

Now that you know how boats float, it's time to make some of your own. The boat models in this book are arranged in order of difficulty. You will learn assembly skills in the first few boats that will be very helpful when you make the more advanced boats. Read carefully through this section. It will give you the foundation you need to build truly amazing paper boats!

TOOLS
These are things you will need to gather before you begin:
- Scissors
- Craft or kitchen utility knife
- Plastic letter opener (or a similar blunt, pointed instrument)
- Ruler
- Model cement-type glue
- Pencil
- Paper clips and small binder clips
- Quarters and nickels for ballast

OPTIONAL TOOLS
- Tweezers
- Waterproof markers
- Toothpicks
- Modeling clay for ballast
- Cutting mat

GETTING STARTED
Before assembling a boat, read through the instructions to get an idea of what you will be doing. This is especially important for boats that have optional parts. Then, remove the appropriate page or pages of waterproof paper from the book. Do this by carefully cutting the page along the straight black line that is close to the binding of the book.

SCORING
Once the page is separated from the book, the first thing to do is to score all the dashed and dotted lines, which are the fold lines. Scoring, or marking a little groove along the lines, will guide your folding. It's easiest to score the lines before cutting out the individual pieces of the boat. Score by laying a ruler alongside the dotted and dashed lines. Run a blunt pointed instrument such as a plastic letter opener alongside the ruler, which will keep the line straight. (If you don't have a plastic letter opener, try a metal letter opener or butter knife, but press it gently so you don't cut the paper.) It's a good idea to practice on a piece of scrap paper first to make sure you don't actually cut right through. It helps to put the piece you're scoring on top of a cutting mat or magazine instead of scoring on a hard surface.

CUTTING
After scoring, carefully cut out all of the parts of your model using a sharp pair of scissors. A craft knife is useful for cutting details and small slits. (When using the craft knife, put the piece on a cutting mat, or on top of a magazine or folded newspaper.) Some of the models have interior areas that will be cut away and discarded. These are shaded in red on the back side of the page. It's best to work from the back of each page, as this is where almost all the cut and fold lines are shown. Each model part is labeled with its part number in a place that won't show when the model is finished. These numbers are referred to in the instructions to help with assembly. Keep the parts you cut out organized according to part number to make assembly easier.

If you accidentally cut a part of the model that shouldn't be cut, you can make an easy repair. Just take a scrap piece of the waterproof paper and glue it like an adhesive bandage on the side of the damaged piece that won't show (usually the side that has less color illustration). In an emergency, you can use a patch of invisible tape, but it may come off after your boat has been in the water for a while.

FOLDING

When the parts are all cut from the sheet you will be able to turn them over to see the markings that show you where to make folds:

– – – – – – Dashed lines show that the paper is folded away from you, making a mountain, with the dashes on top of the crease of the fold.

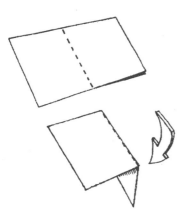

· · · · · · · · · · Dotted lines show that the paper is folded toward you, making a valley, with the dots hidden inside the crease of the fold.

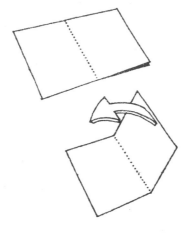

The scoring will make it easier to make a straight fold along the proper fold line, but when you are assembling the model you will have to make each fold go in its proper direction depending on whether the fold lines are dotted or dashed.

CURVING

Some parts of the boats are curved. If you try to curve the parts in your fingers, you may accidentally make creases. The best way to avoid this is to first curve the part around a pencil or thin paintbrush handle. The instructions will tell you when to do this.

COLORED SPOTS

To make assembly easier, many of the tabs and parts of the boats are coded with colored spots. When you have folded the various parts, you will find that the spots meet where the parts are to be glued.

TABS AND SLOTS

As you build your boats, some parts will be attached by tabs that fit into slots. Be careful cutting the slots, which are indicated with short solid lines (on the edges of the hull, for instance). Use a craft knife for the most accurate cut, or carefully push one side of a scissors through the paper to make a slot.

Some of the tabs have curvy shapes that make them fit snugly in the slots. You will fold in the sides of a tab to make it skinny enough to go through the slot. Once the tab fits through the slot, you will open the sides of the tab so it stays in place. Inserting a tab into its slot can be easier if you open the slot a bit with a pointed object, like a straightened-out paper clip.

BALLAST

When you've made your models, you will probably want to float them. Because they are made of light material, they will tend to float high in the water, and some will lean to one side. To overcome this, weight, or ballast, will have to be added. The instructions will tell you how to use quarters, nickels, or modeling clay as ballast in your boats.

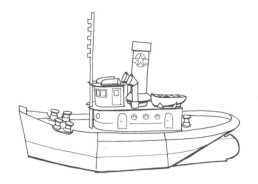

GLUE

Some models require glue, and others do not. It will say at the top of the instruction page whether or not glue is required. You can also use glue on some parts of the non-glue models to ease assembly and make a stronger model.

The glue you will need to stick the waterproof paper and make a water-tight model is "model cement." Model cement can be found in stationery stores or hobby shops. One brand that is distributed widely is Duco Model & Plastic Cement. No matter what glue you use, be sure to read and follow the manufacturer's directions carefully.

When gluing parts together, it often helps to clip them with a paper clip until the glue is dry. This is particularly useful for the pleats on the sides of some of the boats. If paper clips don't fit around a drying pleat, try small binder clips, which are useful for pinching drying parts closed.

FINISHING TOUCHES

When your model is assembled you can color the edges of the paper, which may show as a white line. Do this very carefully with a waterproof marker pen, using a dark color.

BUILDING TIME

The boats are ordered in the book according to level of complexity. Notice the ratings of Easy, Mid-level, and Challenging, which are indicated on the instruction pages by one, two, or three flags.

An estimate of how long it will take to assemble the model is also included with each set of instructions. The estimate is just that, and it can take less or more time to assemble the model. Usually, the more advanced a model is, the longer it takes to assemble, but not always. For instance, the Aircraft Carrier is a Mid-level boat that you will assemble about halfway through the book. The techniques used to build the superstructure on the deck are advanced, but the whole project is not very time consuming. You will have your fabulous Aircraft Carrier in about two to three hours.

Making the models is not like running a race—you don't have to do it all at once. You can stop whenever you like and come back to your boat later. A natural place to take a break is after you have done all the scoring and cutting. There are some models in the book that appear in pairs: the Bark Canoe, the Rowboat, the Offshore Racing Boat, and the Sailboat. After you have built the first model, it will take less time to build the second one.

PLAYING WITH THE MODELS

When you have made your models, they will be so amazing looking, you will want to put them on a shelf, but don't do that! These boats were meant to be played with in the water.

Race your Bark Canoes down a stream and sail your Sailboat across a swimming pool—the sails really work. Reenact the battle between the Civil War ironclads the *Monitor* and the *Merrimack* in your bathtub. The best surprise of all is the last model, the Mississippi Paddle Wheeler. Its paddle wheel really spins. Wind it up and watch it go!

After you have finished playing with your boats for the day, rinse them in fresh water, empty and let dry in a well ventilated space so they'll be ready for their next adventure.

NAUTICAL TERMS

AFT
The direction toward the stern

BALLAST
Weight placed in the hold of a vessel to enhance stability

BEAM
The maximum width of a vessel

BOW
The front end of a vessel

BOW FLAG
Flag at the front end of a vessel

BOWSPRIT
The long spar that extends forward from the bow

BULKHEAD
A wall in a ship

BULWARK
The side of a ship above the upper deck

DECK
A platform on a vessel that covers the hull or forms a floor for its compartments

DECKHOUSE
A superstructure on a ship's upper deck

DRAFT
The depth of the hull that is under the water line

FORWARD
The direction toward the bow

FREEBOARD
The height of the hull above the water

HELM
Used to steer a vessel (a ship's steering wheel or tiller)

HULL
The main structure or shape of the vessel designed to float

KEEL
The center spine of the hull

KNOT
Nautical miles per hour

LINE
Rope, when used aboard a vessel

MAST
A long, vertical pole or spar rising from the keel or deck of a ship, supporting the rigging

MAINSAIL
The principle sail on the main mast of a sailboat

NAUTICAL MILE
1.15 land miles

OVERHEAD
The ceiling, or underside of a deck

PILOTHOUSE
Deckhouse from which the pilot of the vessel steers, also known as wheelhouse

PORT
The left side of a vessel

PORTHOLE
A round opening in the hull or deckhouse of a ship

PORT LIGHT
The glass window in a porthole that can be opened

RUDDER
A vertical blade mounted on the stern, used to steer a vessel

SPAR
A stout pole used to hold rigging; masts, booms, gaffs, and yards are all spars

STARBOARD
The right side of a vessel

STERN
The back end of a vessel

TILLER
A long horizontal handle attached to the rudder, used to turn it left or right

TRANSOM
The planking that forms the stern of a square-ended boat

TRIM
The position of a vessel in water—a properly trimmed boat is floating level in the water

VESSEL
General name for any kind of boat or ship

WHEELHOUSE
Also known as pilothouse, the deckhouse from which a vessel is steered

BARK CANOE

Canoes are one of the oldest and most important boats in the history of water craft, and have been made by people all over the world for thousands of years. The dugout canoe, made by hollowing out a tree trunk, is probably the oldest type of boat ever used.

Dugout canoes are heavy for their size. Canoes made of tree bark are much lighter and can be carried from river to river or lake to lake. For these reasons, bark canoes became extremely popular throughout the world.

WHAT'S THEIR HISTORY?

Bark canoes were perfected by Native Americans long before Europeans crossed the Atlantic Ocean in their ships. Like the native peoples, European explorers used the thousands of lakes and rivers of the continent as roads through the North American wilderness. Bark-covered canoes were the perfect vessels for wilderness travel because they were light, strong, and easy to build and repair with materials found in the woods.

The most common type of canoe used in North America was made from birch bark.

19

The birch tree has a white skin that's strong and stiff, like leather. It can be peeled off a tree in large sections.

HOW WERE THEY MADE?

To make a canoe, a single piece of bark was peeled off a tree. It was then laid out on the ground where the ends were sewn together with the thin roots of spruce trees. The stitching holes were sealed with tar made from boiled tree pitch. Larger canoes needed several sections of bark sewn together. Curved ribs carved from spruce limbs were fitted inside the canoe to give it a strong hull. The ends of the ribs were fastened to long strips of wood that were sewn to the top edges of the bark hull all the way from the bow (front) to the stern (back). Wooden cross-spacers called "thwarts" were then fastened between the sides to keep the canoe from collapsing.

Most canoes were made for two people to paddle, with one kneeling in the front and one in back. Other canoes were large enough to carry a dozen people or more, along with supplies and cargo for long-distance voyaging.

WHAT ARE THEY LIKE TODAY?

The basic design of the traditional canoe was so perfect that they are still made today and still used worldwide. Modern canoes are made of materials such as plastic, aluminum, or fiberglass, and come in a variety of colors. Still, boat builders from two hundred years ago would recognize a modern canoe as the same type of boat they used to navigate the lakes and rivers of the North American wilderness.

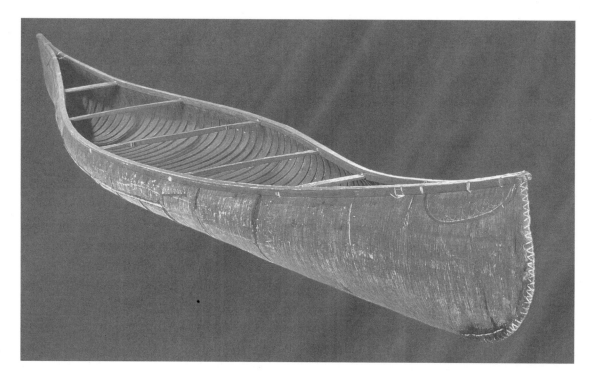

BARK CANOE ASSEMBLY

About one hour
Glue optional
Models on pages 81–82

There are two of these models, and
although they look different, they
are exactly the same shape, and
therefore these instructions apply
to both. These models may be built
without glue, though you may use
glue to assemble them if you wish.
The last section of the instructions
will tell you how to use glue.

STEP 1: SCORING AND CUTTING

Cut one of the models from the page,
and score all the parts where indicated.
You will need to look at both sides of
the pages to see all the markings.
Some of the fold lines are shown in
white. Cut the six slots on Part 1 (three
on each side, indicated on the front of
the page). Next, turn the page over and
cut the two slots where indicated on
the small, red, triangular area at each
end of the canoe. Cut out the four
parts of the canoe. First study both
sides of the page. Some areas are not
colored, but the outline is indicated in
black. Cut around the outside of each
part, including the outlined areas.

STEP 2: FOLDING

Carefully fold the creases where indicated. Next, with the inside of the
model facing upward, fold one end of
Part 1 up (see Diagram A). Next, fold
the center part of the fold outward,
following the fold lines. You should now
have a W-shaped fold. Gradually
increase the sharpness of the fold,
squeezing the end of the canoe
together to a point (see Diagrams B
and C, which show this from different
angles).

Diagram A

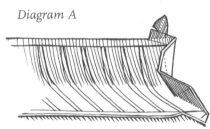

Diagram B

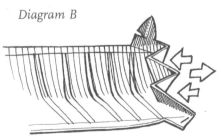

Diagram C

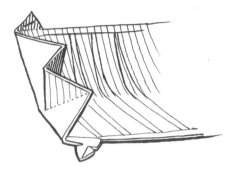

STEP 3: HULL FINISHING

At each end of the canoe (Part 1),
there is a small, red, triangular area.
Fold this down (with the red underneath) to form a small flat area at the
end of the canoe. Now fold in the flap
on the yellow-spot tab, and curve the
tab around your finger. Curving this tab
will make it easier to insert, and will
hold the flap down while you push the
tab into its slot. Now enlarge the
yellow-spot slot slightly by poking a
sharp object (such as the end of your
scissors) into it. Now study Diagram D,
and insert the tab into its slot, holding
the end of the canoe together. When
the tab is fully inserted the flap should
pop open, locking the tab in position. If
the flap doesn't open, insert a pointed
object (such as a letter opener) into the
slot beside the tab to lever the flap open.

Diagram D

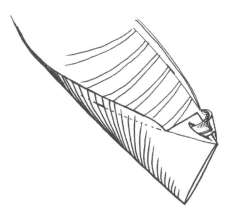

STEP 5: BALLAST

Your canoe is now almost ready to sail, but you will need some ballast so it floats upright. The best thing to use is a small bit of modeling clay (about the size of a small marble) fixed in the bottom of the canoe at each end. You can even use a couple of small pebbles or any other small, heavy object. Happy canoeing!

DIRECTIONS FOR ASSEMBLY WITH GLUE

Follow the instructions for cutting and folding the canoe, Steps 1 and 2. You can now stick the bow together, applying a little glue to the inside of the folds at the bow. When the glue is dry, cut the yellow-spot tab off the small triangular area at each end and simply stick the small triangular area on top of the larger triangle, forming a small flat area at each end of the canoe. The rest of the assembly is the same as the no-glue version.

STEP 4: STRUTS

See Diagram E for how the struts will appear in the finished model. Fold the side edges of the canoe down and make a sharp crease along the top edge. Now fold them back up again. Take the center strut (Part 2) and fold the sides of the strut down (white side underneath). Fold the sides of the end tabs up. Insert the tabs into the center slots, one on each side. Unfold the tab sides to lock the strut in position. Next, fix the two end struts (Parts 3A and 3B) in the same way. To position the struts correctly, put the narrower side toward the ends of the boat. Fold the top edge of the canoe down again. The ends of the tabs will stick out, and you can cut off the parts that show. Now curve and crease the top edge of your canoe so that you have a smooth curve from end to end.

Diagram E

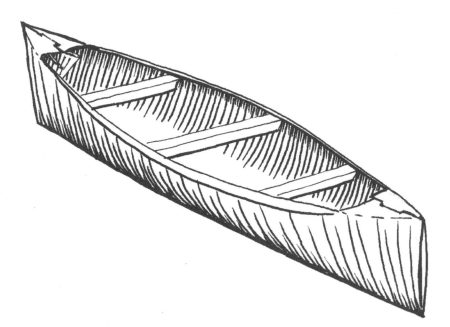

I f you've been anywhere near water, you've probably seen or been in a rowboat. They're basic, very popular, and very important. Rowboats come in various shapes and sizes, and are designed to fit a lot of different needs. Along with canoes, they're the most common types of boats around.

HOW DO ROWBOATS WORK?

Rowboats are simple. They have a basic hull, a seat, and at least one set of oars. The oars pass through oarlocks, which hold the oars in position and are fastened to the top edge of a boat's sides. The rower faces the back of the boat and pulls the oar grips forward, pulling the blade at the end of the oar through the water and providing the power stroke. On the recovery stroke, the rower lifts the blades out of the water and brings them forward, in position for another power stroke. To turn the boat, the rower rows harder on the oar opposite the direction the rower wants to go.

WHAT SIZE ARE THEY?

Rowboats can be big or small. Some of the largest rowboats are the huge lifeboats carried on ocean liners. In an emergency, one of these can carry seventy-five people or more.

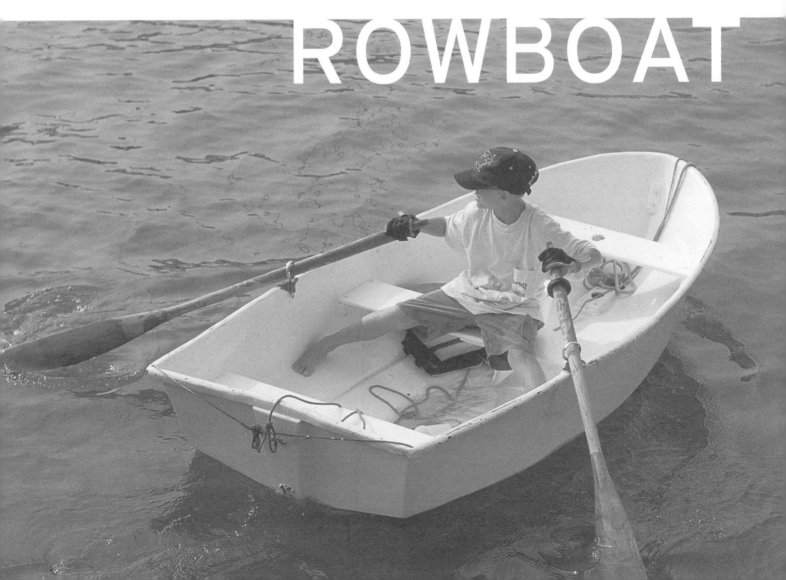

ROWBOAT

seaworthy in large ocean swells even when loaded with hundreds of pounds of fish.

ROWBOATS TO THE RESCUE
Special rowboats, called surf boats, are used by lifesaving teams. These boats are designed to be launched from beaches to rescue sailors stranded on sinking ships. Surf-boat teams take great pride in their ability to row through even the roughest waves to reach a shipwreck as quickly as possible.

ROWBOATS AT WAR
The largest rowboats in history were the Roman and Greek galleys, which were powered by as many as 1,800 oarsmen! The Viking longboats are also among the most important rowboats in history. Their huge sailboats could travel great distances. But it was the oars on the vessels that powered the Vikings into shallow bays and up rivers where they could attack villages. This advantage helped the Vikings to spread their influence across Europe and Asia.

ROWBOATS IN COMPETITION
Rowing crews have always challenged each other to races, whether in dorys or surf boats. Today, rowing competitions are held with many different kinds of boats around the world. The most advanced type of racing rowboats are the long, thin racing shells used by university teams in England and the United States.

From large to small, sophisticated to simple, there is probably no type of vessel more popular than the rowboat.

Larger rowboats have many rowers with several pairs of oars, and most have a "coxswain," someone who steers the boat with a rudder and tiller. The rudder is a blade that sticks down in the water at the back of the boat and turns it right or left. The tiller is a long, wooden handle used to move the rudder. The coxswain faces forward and can see which way the boat is going. To keep everyone rowing together at the proper speed, the coxswain calls out: "stroke, stroke."

The smallest rowboats are called dinghies and are often carried on small sailboats. When the sailboat is anchored, dinghies are used to get to shore.

ROWBOATS AT WORK
One of the most famous types of rowboats was the double-ended dory used by fishermen on the Grand Banks off Canada's northeastern coast. Dozens of these boats were launched from large schooners (typically, a two-masted sailing vessel) to set fishing lines. These boats had to be very

ROWBOAT ASSEMBLY

About one to two hours
Glue required
Models on pages 83-86

STEP 1: SCORING AND CUTTING

Score and cut out both of the pieces. Fold all creases where marked. Note that some of the fold marks are shown in white on the colored inside of the boat, and that there are two small areas that will be cut out and discarded. These are shown by red shading on the back of the page.

STEP 2: SEATS

See Diagram A. Fold the middle and front seats on Part 1 into box shapes, and glue tabs onto the pale green areas. The small triangular areas at the bow should be glued into box shapes, bringing the blue spots together. Fold and glue the stern seat and transom assembly as shown, gluing the tab onto the green area.

Diagram B

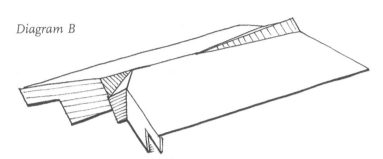

STEP 3: FOLDING HULL

See Diagram B (seats not shown for clarity). Turn the hull over, and carefully increase the angle of the folds at the bow. The center section should fold inward as you bring the sides together, until the yellow spots meet. Diagram B shows the folding at an early stage. When the edges meet, open up the fold and apply glue to the inside (pale green) part of the folded area. (The triangular "boxes" at the bow and seat assembly stick out at this stage.) It helps to hold the bow together with paper clips while the glue dries. When the glue is dry, put your finger inside the bow and open it up to a point.

STEP 4: KEEL AND TRANSOM

Apply glue to the inside of the keel (this is the triangular area along the bottom of the boat, marked "X" on Diagram A.) Fold, bringing the red spots together. Hold with paper clips. Fold the transom (Part 2). Note that the four bottom tabs are colored brown; the fold lines for these tabs are white. Fix the transom to the stern of the boat by gluing the tabs to the inside of the hull, starting with the middle tabs. Make sure the transom is straight.

Diagram A

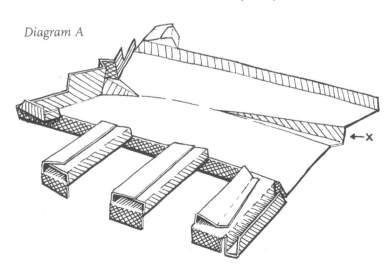

←X

Diagram C

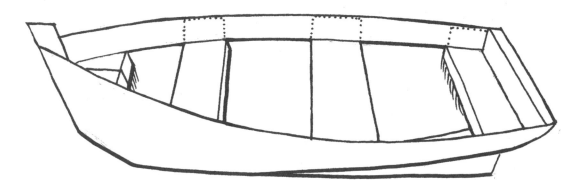

STEP 5: FINAL ASSEMBLY

See Diagram C. First, fold in the left-hand side flap (the one with seats attached), bringing the purple spots together. Now, open and apply glue. Refold, and smooth the inside down, pressing out any bumps or irregularities. Fold seats into position and glue the end of each seat onto the green square. Apply glue under the right-hand flap, then fold it down on top of the seat tabs. Now look at the boat from above. The sides should curve smoothly from bow to stern. Straighten out any kinks or irregularities before the glue is fully hardened.

Glue the transom flap down on the outside of the transom, bringing the orange spots together. Then glue the two triangular "box" sections at the bow onto the center spine. (See Diagram C.)

STEP 6: FLOAT-TESTING

You can now float-test your boat. First, test for leaks. The easiest way to test is to fill the boat with water, and check carefully to see if any escapes. Any leaks can be repaired using a blob of glue on the inside after you empty your boat and dry it thoroughly. Apply the glue very carefully, so that it doesn't spoil the appearance of your boat. Now, float your boat; you will find that it leans to one side. To correct this, you will need to add ballast to the inside. Modeling clay is ideal for this, or small stones. You can tuck the ballast under the bow and stern ends of the boat. Add ballast until your boat floats straight.

OFFSHORE RACING BOAT

What has 2,000 horsepower and thunders across the water at over 170 miles per hour? An Offshore-Class racing boat on its way to victory! As long as there have been engines and boats, there have been people ready to prove which boat is fastest. As members of the American Power Boat Association, offshore racing boats compete in several categories determined by size, hull shape, and engine type. Some have inboard engines, some have outboards. Some have V-shaped hulls, while others are high-tech catamarans (a boat with twin hulls). Some are factory-built family runabouts, and some, such as the giant Unlimiteds and Offshore-Class boats, are multimillion-dollar, custom-built monsters.

WHAT'S THEIR HISTORY?

Organized powerboat racing began in 1904 with an international race across the 22-mile-wide English Channel. Offshore racing soon spread to the United States with important races on both the West and East coasts. By the late 1950s, the golden age of offshore powerboat racing was in high gear.

HOW DO THEY WORK?

The Offshore-Class boats, designed to compete on the open ocean, are between 26 and 39 feet long. The large Class B boats have twin inboard engines and require a crew of three seated in an open cockpit. The team is headed by the driver, who must use all of his or her strength and concentration to steer the boat as it bounces over the waves. The engines are controlled by the throttle operator, who adjusts the speed and monitors performance and fuel consumption. To keep the boat on course, the third team member is the navigator, who uses the high-tech Global Positioning System (GPS) to find out exactly where the boat is and how far it is to the next mark.

During offshore races, the team competes against other boats but must also battle the wind, waves, and weather on the open ocean.

WHAT ARE THEY LIKE TODAY?

The sport has continued to grow under the authority of the American Power Boat Association, which now has over 7,000 members. From the amateur weekend competitor to the professional offshore teams, powerboat racing has speed, skill, screaming engines, and all the excitement you could ask for!

OFFSHORE RACING BOAT ASSEMBLY

About two hours
Glue optional
Models on pages 87–92

There are two of these boats. They are exactly the same design, but have very different color schemes. They can be assembled without glue, but if you decide to use glue see the notes in the instructions. Note that some of the parts for these boats appear on a separate sheet of waterproof paper, along with parts of the Rescue Lifeboat.

STEP 1: SCORING AND CUTTING

Score and cut out all the parts of the boat. If using glue for construction, DO NOT cut the nine slits on each side of the hull (Part 1). Instead cut seven small V-shaped cuts into each edge as indicated in green on the plan side of the page.

Diagram A

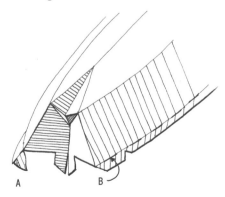

A   B

STEP 2: BOW

Crease the hull (Part 1) where indicated. Start folding the bow section, as shown in Diagram A. The small kite-shaped area folds inward, bringing the green spots together. Finally, squeeze the bow together to form a good sharp point. If using glue, apply a little to the inside of the bow fold to hold the two halves tightly together. Next, fold in the triangular area at the bow to form a small deck section. If not using glue, fold in the flaps of the orange-spot tab (indicated "A" on the diagram) and insert into its corresponding slot (orange, and marked "B" on the diagram). Unfold the tab flaps with a sharp instrument, securing the bow triangle. If using glue, cut off the orange-spot tab and glue the triangular deck piece to the folded edge of the opposite side.

STEP 3: STERN

Fold in the corners of the stern, bringing the red spots together. (These areas may be glued, if you are using glue.) You will now have a triangular pocket inside the hull. (See Diagram B, left-hand side.) Now fold one of the long rectangular tabs, bringing the yellow spots together; finally the blue triangular part folds underneath the pocket, holding the stern together. (See the right-hand side of Diagram B.) The small tab in the middle of the stern folds forward to a horizontal position.

Diagram B

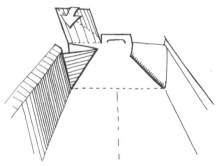

STEP 4: DECK AND SEATS

Part 2 (the seats) is complex; there are many folds and six long slits, but the seats are quite easy to form if you use a pencil and thread it between the slits, as shown in Diagram C. When you have the shape roughly formed, withdraw the pencil and squeeze to sharpen the creases. Fold the rest of the part to form the floor and control panel as shown on Diagrams C and E.

Next, fold in the side flaps on the front tabs (marked with red spots) and insert into the slots marked with red spots on the deck (Part 3). It helps to pull the tabs gently from below. Next, push the cockpit assembly into the deck opening, leaving the seat and rear (green spot) tabs outside. Finally, insert the green-spot tabs into their corresponding slots on the deck and make a last check, comparing the assembly with Diagram E.

Diagram C

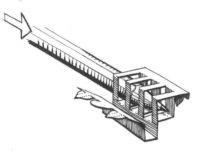

STEP 5: SPRAY SCREEN

Fold the spray screen (Part 4) and fix to deck, matching the color spots.

STEP 6: FIXING DECK TO HULL

First, fold in the flaps on the sides of the front (green-spot) tab on the deck (Part 3). Turn the deck upside down and insert the tab into its matching slot on the hull (Part 1). Unfold the locking flaps, then fold the deck back into position. If you are using glue, apply it to the side tabs on the top of the hull, one side at a time, and fix the deck carefully into position, taking care to form a neat join along the top edge of the hull.

Diagram D

IF YOU ARE USING THE NO-GLUE SYSTEM, PROCEED AS FOLLOWS:
Pull back and upward on the deck, curving it upward as shown in Diagram D. Insert the first "leaf" tab (with yellow spot) into its slot in the top of the hull. Feed carefully into the slot, and at the same time lower the deck into position. Holding the deck in place, repeat on the opposite side. Now proceed to the red-spot tab and so on, matching the tabs with their slots until you reach the blue-spot locking tab. Fold in the sides of the tab and insert it into its slot to lock the deck in place. Now gently pull the deck from the stern end and pinch along both edges of the deck to form a neat crease.

STEP 7: ENGINE COVERS

Make very sharp creases along the scored lines on Part 5, the engine covers. See Diagram E for the shape required. Using a sharp point, ease open the slots in the deck. Now feed the yellow tabs of the engine covers into their corresponding slots on the deck, followed by the other tabs, forming the shape of the engine covers as you go. Finally, insert the central deck flap at the stern (marked with a yellow spot), and you are ready to race!

Diagram E

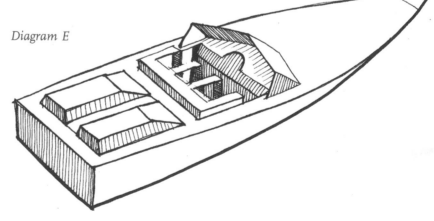

MAHOGANY
RUNABOUT

Imagine yourself boarding a 1950s Chris Craft Capri. Look at the hull of the boat. It's made of a beautiful, dark-reddish wood called mahogany that is coated with thirteen to seventeen layers of clear varnish. The wood becomes so smooth and shiny that it is known as "brightwork." Step on board and sit in the open cockpit behind a cool wraparound windshield. There's a steering wheel like the one you might find in a car, and lots of shiny, chrome-plated trim. You can't see the engine because it's hidden under a curved rear deck, but it's powerful. Take the boat for a spin and you'll slice through the water at 40 mph. Race with it, or use it for water skiing. Even standing still, it's incredibly beautiful and exciting. No wonder this classic wooden runabout was king of the water from the 1920s to the 1950s.

WHAT'S THEIR HISTORY?

Runabouts were developed almost a hundred years ago, when lightweight gasoline engines began to replace heavy steam propulsion in small boats. But people wanted more than rowboats with engines, so boat builders in the United States and Canada starting making beautiful wooden powerboats called "utility launches," used for carrying people and supplies to and from their cabins on resort lakes.

During the 1920s—known as the "Roaring Twenties"—people were fascinated with speed and glamour. Race cars and airplanes set new world records, and high-speed motorboat racing became very popular. Raceboat drivers were heroes and everyone wanted a fast, shiny boat. So the builders began to offer a new class of pleasure craft called the Runabout.

When the United States entered World War II in 1941, wooden boat companies focused on building vessels for the U.S. Navy. But when the war ended, more Americans than ever had the time and money to spend on boating. Boat builders could hardly keep up with demand. Mahogany was expensive however, and skilled workers were hard to find. Builders began to use a new material called fiberglass. With this reinforced plastic material, thousands of boats were made from molds on a factory production line. By the early 1960s, the age of the custom-built wooden runabout had ended.

WHAT ARE THEY LIKE TODAY?

Today, most speedboats are made of high-tech fiberglass and look like floating race cars. Recently, though, some people have grown tired of mass-produced boats that all look the same. A few companies have begun making copies of the classic runabouts. Although they're built with modern materials the new boats look and feel as thrilling as the great wooden runabouts of the past.

MAHOGANY RUNABOUT ASSEMBLY

About two hours
Glue optional
Model on pages 93–94

STEP 1: SCORING AND CUTTING

Score and cut out all the pieces of the runabout.

STEP 2: HULL

See Diagram A. Turn hull (Part 1) upside down (red side upward). Fold the bow and sides inward. There will be a fold across the bow, forming a square section.

Diagram A

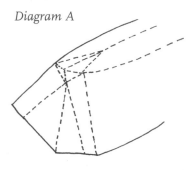

STEP 3: BOW

See Diagram B. Squeeze bow halves together, and then tuck in the little triangle to form the curve of the front of the boat. Fold gradually, checking that folds form properly on the scored lines. The triangle folds in half, bringing the green spots together. If you want to use glue, the pocket formed inside the bow (and the smaller green-spot area) may be glued together.

Diagram B

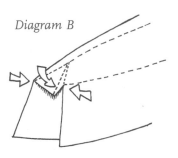

STEP 4: FINISHING BOW

Now turn the model right side up. At the bow there is a triangular pocket that you have just formed. Fold this pocket in half, bringing the yellow spots together, and following the fold lines. Now insert the blue tabs into the pocket with blue edges to secure the bow. Squeeze the bow together between your finger and thumb to form really sharp creases. Now fold the triangular flap over. Fold in the sides of the orange-spot locking tab, and insert into the orange-spot slot on opposite side of bow. Make sure the tab is fully inserted; if necessary use a pointed object to help unfold the flaps of the tab.

Diagram C

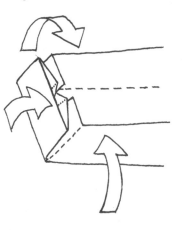

STEP 5: STERN

For the stern, fold the gusset sections inside the hull (see Diagram C), bringing corners of the stern and yellow spots together. Now see Diagram D, and look inside the hull. You will see the creases for a second fold, and the shaded area in the diagram. Fold this area toward you and upward to bring the orange spots together, and the opening to deck level. If you are using glue, these folds may be glued together. Now tuck the red-spot tab into the red-edged area, holding the stern together.

Diagram D

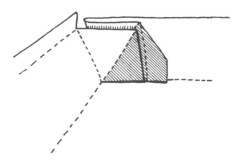

STEP 6: DECK

Fold the deck (Part 2) where indicated. (Be sure you've cut out and discarded the two small areas indicated by red shading.) Fold the dashboard into shape, paying particular attention to the direction of the folds. There is a step fold to form the steering wheel support. (See Diagram E.)

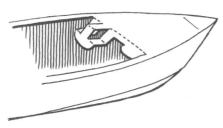

Diagram E

Note: If you are using glue, all the leaf-shaped tabs may be cut off, and the deck simply glued to the side tabs on the hull.

Diagram G

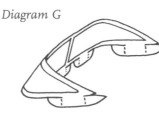

Diagram H

STEP 7: FIXING DECK TO HULL

To attach the deck to the hull, start at the bow. (See Diagram F.) Fold in the edges of the red-spot locking tab. Insert into the red-spot slot at the bow. (Make sure the deck is the right way up!) Pull back and upward gently on the deck (see diagram) until the point of the yellow-spot leaf-shaped tab can be inserted into its slot. Feed carefully into the slot and at the same time lower the deck into position. Hold the deck in position on this side, repeat on the opposite side. Now proceed to the red-spot tabs and so on, matching the colors of the tabs with their slots until you reach the blue-spot locking tab. Now fold the locking flaps in and insert. If you carefully pull the seat assembly up you will be able to reach inside the hull and unfold the locking tabs to hold the deck down. Now gently pull the deck from the stern, and pinch along both edges of the deck to form a neat crease. Finally, fold the edges of the yellow-spot locking tab in at the stern; insert into the slot in the stern and push down to lock in place.

Diagram F

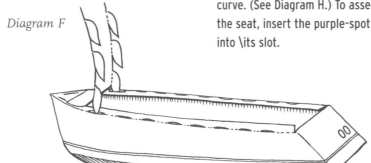

STEP 8: WINDSHIELD

To install the windshield (Part 3), first curve it carefully around a thin pencil. (See Diagram G.)

Fold the tabs. Insert the green-spot tabs first into the slots in the front deck. (It may help if you open the slots slightly with a pointed instrument, such as a straightened paper clip.) Next, insert the blue-spot tabs. Note: These tabs pass through slots both in the deck and the hull top.

STEP 9: FRONT SEAT

To assemble the front seat (Part 4), fold where indicated. Curve the seat top around a pencil to form a smooth curve. (See Diagram H.) To assemble the seat, insert the purple-spot tab into \its slot.

STEP 10: JOINING SEATS

To join the front and back seats, insert the purple-spot tabs on back seats into the purple-spot slots on the front seats. Carefully bend the rear seat, while pushing the front seat assembly into the hull. The projections on the side of the front seat will have to be carefully bent to get them under the deck. The top of the seats should stick slightly above the level of the deck.

Diagram I

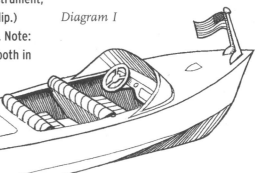

STEP 11: FLAGPOLE

Fold the flagpole and navigation light (Part 5). Insert the tabs into the slots at the bow (you may need to enlarge the slots first with your craft knife). Finally, place the steering wheel (Part 6). The little flaps fold behind the projection on the dashboard.

COAST GUARD BOAT

Maybe you've seen them, cruising the waters, white boats with a diagonal orange stripe across their bow and black lettering on their sides that reads Coast Guard. But did you know that the U.S. Coast Guard is the largest rescue organization in the world? Or that on an average day the Coast Guard saves fourteen lives?

And that's not all the Coast Guard does; it's also responsible for maintaining navigational aids like buoys, lighthouses, and channel markers, protecting the marine environment, and leading the fight against smuggling illegal drugs on the water.

IS A BOAT AS IMPORTANT AS A CUTTER?

The Coast Guard classifies all of its vessels that are 65 feet or longer as "cutters," and all smaller vessels as "boats." But don't think that the word boat makes these high-tech vessels any less important or capable.

The 41-foot Utility Boat, for example, is designed for search-and-rescue and port security operations in moderate sea conditions. Utility boats (UTBs) also carry out safe boating and pollution inspections.

Along the thousands of miles of coastline protected by the Coast Guard, hundreds of UTBs, motor lifeboats, and fast coastal interceptors are ready to spring into action 24 hours a day.

WHAT ARE THE UTBs LIKE?

The UTB's hull is made of aluminum and its deckhouse is made of fiberglass. This combination results in a lightweight yet incredibly strong vessel able to sprint to any emergency at nearly 30 miles per hour. At its efficient cruise speed of 18 knots, the 41-foot UTB has a range of 300 miles (the distance it can travel before turning back for fuel). A nautical mile, or knot, equals 1.15 land miles. Nautical miles are used on the oceans, and regular land miles are used on rivers and inland lakes, including the Great Lakes.

The crew of these versatile boats consists of an engineer, deck hand, and coxswain—the person who steers the boat. UTBs are guided on their missions by the latest navigational aids, including radar and the GPS satellite network. But UTBs carry more than their crew. They're designed to hold up to twenty-two people rescued at sea.

Together with other boats, cutters, rescue helicopters, and search aircraft of the U.S. Coast Guard, UTBs help keep coastlines safe, day and night.

COAST GUARD BOAT ASSEMBLY

About three hours
Glue optional
Model on pages 95–96

This boat can be assembled without glue, but if you decide to use glue for assembly, instructions are included throughout. The radar mast on the superstructure (Part 3) is quite intricate and you may decide not to include it in your model. This part may be removed by cutting though the blue line on the plan side of the page.

STEP 1: SCORING AND CUTTING

Score and cut out all the parts where indicated. If using glue, do not cut the slits along the sides of the hull. Instead, make five small V-shaped cuts indicated in green on the back (plan) side of the page.

Diagram A

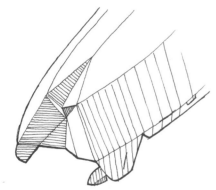

STEP 2: HULL

Crease the hull (Part I) where indicated. Start folding the bow section as shown in Diagram A. Fold the small kite-shaped area inward, bringing the green spots together. Next, squeeze the bow to form a good sharp point. If using glue, apply a little to the inside of the bow fold to hold the two halves of the bow together. Next, fold in the gray triangular area to form a small deck section at the bow. Now fold in the flap of the orange-spot tab and insert into the corresponding orange-spot slot to secure. The flap on this tab may not open by itself, in which case you should ease it open with a pointed instrument.

STEP 3: STERN

Fold in the corners of the stern, bringing the red spots together. (These areas may be glued if you wish.) You will now have a triangular pocket inside the hull. See Diagram B, left-hand side. Now fold down one of the long rectangular tabs, bringing the yellow spots together, and finally fold the blue triangular flap underneath the pocket, to hold the stern together. See the right-hand side of Diagram B.

Diagram B

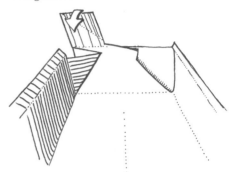

STEP 4: DECK

Be sure that you have cut the slits and cut out and discarded the red-shaded area in the center, leaving a rectangular hole. Crease and fold down the petal-shaped tabs along the side of the deck (Part 2). If you are using glue, the seven petal tabs may be cut off. For both types of assembly, fold in the flaps of the front (green-spot) tab on the deck. Now turn the deck upside down and insert the tab into its matching slot on the front of the hull. Unfold the locking flaps, and then fold the deck back into position. If you are using glue, apply glue to the side tabs on the top of the hull one side at a time and fix the deck carefully into position, taking care to form a neat joining along the top edge of the hull. If you are using the no-glue method, proceed as follows: Study Diagram C. Now pull back and upward on the deck, curving it as shown in Diagram C. Insert the first leaf tab (with a yellow spot) into its slot in the top of the hull. Feed it carefully into the slot and at the same time lower the deck into position. Holding the deck in place, repeat on the opposite side. Now proceed to the red-spot tabs and so on, matching the tabs with their slots until you reach the blue-spot locking tab. Fold this in and insert into its slot to lock the deck in place. Finally, pinch along the edge joint between the deck and side of the boat, and smooth out any bumps or bulges to tidy up the appearance of the joint.

Diagram D

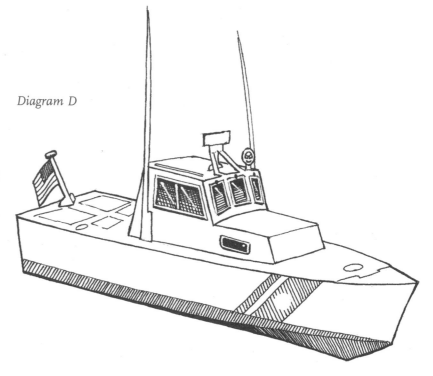

Diagram C

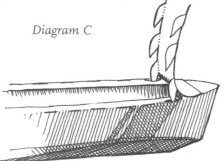

STEP 5: SUPERSTRUCTURE

See Diagram D to get an idea of what this section will look like when finished. First, crease the superstructure (Part 3) where indicated. (Note that there are four small areas indicated by red shading that should have been cut out and discarded.) To assemble the superstructure, first insert the yellow- and orange-spot tabs into their slots, forming the lower front section of the superstructure. Next, insert the small green-spot tab into its slit to form the front of the wheelhouse. You can probably see at this stage how the rest of the superstructure fits together, but don't assemble it just yet.

STEP 6: FIXING SUPERSTRUCTURE

First, fold the flaps on the blue-spot tabs. Now insert the tabs into their corresponding slits in the deck. (It will help if you first enlarge these slits with a pointed instrument.) Next, insert the purple-spot tab, followed by the three tabs on the port (left) side of the deck. Next, fix the large green-spot tab, securing the roof. If you have retained the radar mast assembly, carefully bend back and insert the central tab into its slot on the roof (pull slightly to one side, insert, and pull to center). See Diagram D for a guide to how it should look. You can now fix the back of the wheelhouse in place by inserting the central tab into the deck and fixing the large red-spot tab.

STEP 7: FLAGPOLE, RADIO MASTS

Fold the flagpole (Part 4) where indicated. Fix it in place on the stern, bending the two little locking tabs and inserting them into their slots (see Diagram D). Finally, cut out the two radio masts (Parts 5A and 5B) and fix in place on the sides of the superstructure. You will need glue or a little tape to attach these parts.

RESCUE LIFEBOAT

If you're in danger at sea off the coast of the United Kingdom or Republic of Ireland, your life may depend on the local village librarian, auto mechanic, butcher, sheep farmer, or weekend sailor. But don't worry, you'll be in very good hands indeed: Your rescue crew will be members of the Royal National Lifeboat Institution (RNLI). They are some of the best-trained and highly motivated lifesavers in the world, equipped with state-of-the-art rescue vessels like the Severn-Class all-weather lifeboat.

HOW DOES THE RNLI WORK?

The RNLI is an all-volunteer service that has been responsible for saving lives along Britain and Ireland's coastlines for over 175 years. Operating from 224 stations, the RNLI saves more than 1,500 lives each year.

When a vessel is in trouble, the Coast Guard calls the nearest lifeboat station. The volunteer crew is alerted with pagers. They instantly drop whatever they are doing and rush to the lifeboat station. Here they quickly change into survival suits and board the waiting lifeboat. At some stations the boats are kept at docks, while at others, smaller boats can be launched down ramps. The crews strap themselves into the water-tight cabins and the boats head out to sea.

The entire RNLI system is supported by public donation. The volunteer crews serve together for many years in their own home

waters. This strong team spirit and local experience, combined with intense, nationally standardized training and the best equipment, create one of the greatest maritime rescue services in the world.

WHAT ARE THE LIFEBOATS LIKE?

The RNLI designs and builds their own fleet of over ten different types of lifeboat, from small inflatables for use on in-shore waters, to the giant Severn- and Trent-Class all-weather lifeboats, which are more like miniature ships than boats. These powerful vessels, made of heavily reinforced fiberglass, can withstand the worst conditions the North Sea can dish out. They can race to the rescue at 25 knots or fight their way through 20-foot waves to reach a vessel in distress, up to 50 miles offshore, guided by radar and GPS satellite network navigation. Their high bows are made to cut through mountainous seas, and their sides are swept close to the water to make it easier to pull survivors aboard. For operating close to shore, their propellers are completely protected so they will not be damaged even if the boat is bounced off the bottom in heavy surf. Capable of rolling all the way over and automatically turning themselves right side up again, these tough all-weather boats are some of the most capable vessels afloat.

RESCUE LIFEBOAT ASSEMBLY

About four hours
Glue required
Model on pages 97–98 and 91–92

STEP 1: SCORING AND CUTTING

Score along the dashed and dotted lines and cut out all the pieces. Note that there is a line of extra-big white dashes at the edge of the deck (on the colored side of Part 2). This is NOT a cut or fold line; it is a part of the design.

STEP 2: HULL

Form creases where indicated on the hull (Part 1). You will notice that the bow has a kite-shaped area, similar to the Offshore Racing Boat models. Carefully press the bow together forming ever-sharper creases, bringing the green spots together; then glue the bow together, forming a triangular gusset inside. Now glue the two small triangular tabs at the top of the bow, bringing the dark orange spots together.

Diagram A

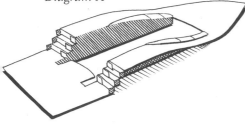

Next, fold the stern together, forming a triangular gusset in each corner and bringing the large red spots together. Glue the triangular flaps into the stern.

STEP 3: DECK

Note that there are four small areas marked with red shading on the deck (Part 2); cut these out and discard. Don't forget to cut the white slit indicated in the center of this part. Next, fold the deck. Make sure that you form especially sharp creases on the steps at the side of the deck. Now refer to Diagram A, which shows the deck assembly upside down, and the general Diagram D, which shows the model completed. If you fold the deck as indicated, you will find the shape beginning to emerge. Start gluing as follows: First, stick the two yellow rectangular areas together, pulling the front and back parts of the deck together. Next, stick the outside of the steps together, folding the tabs over each other to form the corners of the steps, matching the colored spots as you go. Next, glue the inner tabs on each side of the inner deck.

STEP 4: HULL REINFORCEMENT

Crease the hull reinforcement strut (Part 3) where indicated and scored. Glue the yellow spots together to form a triangular tube. Fold the four end tabs outward and finally stick in place inside the deck assembly, pointed-side upward, matching the blue and red spots.

STEP 5: FIXING DECK TO HULL

Apply glue to the two blue-spot tabs on the hull and to the outer end of the steps on the starboard (right) side of the deck. Fix the deck corner onto the hull, noting that the position of the steps is indicated inside the hull, with the step edges shown by a blue line. When dry, apply glue and fix the corresponding area on the port (left) side of the hull. When dry, apply glue to the next three tabs and fix the center section of the deck in place. Finally, glue the remaining tabs and fix, joining the deck at the bow.

STEP 6: SUPERSTRUCTURE

See Diagram B. Crease the superstructure (Part 4). Note that the two areas indicated by red shading are to be discarded. Next, start by gluing the wheelhouse front in place, fixing the blue-spot tab. It helps if you temporarily fold back the wheelhouse roof, indicated by a red square, to make this join. When dry, fold the wheelhouse roof forward, apply a small amount of glue to each side of the roof and fix onto the two small rectangular areas (indicated by a green spot). Now fold the three window tabs down and stick to the front of the wheelhouse. Next, stick the lower wheelhouse front in place; this is indicated by a blue spot. Then stick the two rectangular tabs (green spot) at the back of the wheelhouse, then the box-shaped rear extensions of the superstructure (red and yellow spots), and finally the front lower wall of the superstructure.

Diagram B

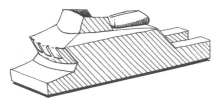

STEP 7: FRONT LOWER ROOF

Fold Part 5 where indicated. Test-fit this part, matching up the green-, red-, and orange-colored spots. Fitting is easiest if the part is inserted from below, as there is a short extension underneath the wheelhouse front that overlays this piece. When you are satisfied with the fit, apply glue to the tabs and fix.

STEP 8: UPPER BRIDGE AND MAST

The upper bridge (Part 6) is quite complex in shape. There are two versions; one eliminates the radio mast and is therefore simpler to make. If you want to make the simpler version, cut away and discard the center black section of Part 6, leaving the two orange outer sections. When you have cut them, fix them together (the blue spots meet up) and glue in place on top of the super-structure as indicated in Diagram B. If you go for the complex version, note that there are five small shaded areas to be cut out and discarded. Be particu-larly careful to follow the cutting lines closely. When you have cut the part, fold the small box-like structure in the

middle into shape, bringing the red spots together. Glue. Next, curve the mast assembly into shape. Refer to Diagram D for the shape. Glue the blue-spot tab, holding the upper bridge assembly together, but don't fix the complete assembly in place until you have finished it.

STEP 9: FIXING SUPERSTRUCTURE

See Diagram D. Test-fit the superstruc-ture before gluing. Note that the orange superstructure fits over the outside of the dark blue flaps on the deck. Apply glue to the inside bottom edge of the superstructure and fix in place on the deck. Next, fix the upper bridge and mast assembly in place on the super-structure. See Diagram D.

STEP 10: INFLATABLE DINGHY

See Diagram C. The dinghy (Part 7) is not essential to the model. If you decide to make it, proceed as follows:

Diagram C

First, form the crease where indicated. The sides of this part are curved, and you should form the curves around a pencil. The shape of the dinghy will gradually emerge, and soon you will see how the sides fix together. The joins are indicated by colored spots, and it's important to stick the overlaps so that the white areas are exactly covered. The spot tabs should be fixed in the following order: blue, green, red, purple, brown, and then white. The finished dinghy is shown (upside down) in Diagram C. Finally, stick the dinghy (open side down) on the upper deck behind the upper bridge.

Diagram D

SAILBOAT

Who knows when the first prehistoric sailor stretched an animal hide between two poles to get a boost from the wind? Since then, sails have been added to nearly every kind of vessel ever made. Unlike human-powered boats, or even boats that have engines, sailboats have a limitless source of power. Even if the wind dies down for a while, there will always be more. The wind has powered countless adventurous voyages—from toy sailboats across small ponds to great, tall ships carrying dozens of sails around the globe.

HOW DO SAILBOATS WORK?

It's easy to understand how wind can fill a sail and push it along in the direction it is blowing. This is called "downwind sailing." But how do sailboats sail toward the wind? You can't sail directly into the wind, but you can sail on an angle toward the wind. Because sails act like airplane wings, they can create "lift" as the air moves around their curved shapes. Lift is generated when air flows faster over the curved top surface of a wing or sail and creates lower air pressure there than on the bottom. This lifts an airplane up and "lifts" a sailboat forward. To sail into the

wind, a sailboat must tack (or zigzag) back and forth. Alternating sides of the sails create the lift that allows you to make windward progress, meaning you progress on a course toward the direction from which the wind is blowing.

WHAT'S THEIR HISTORY?

Sailing ships enabled early explorers to cross oceans and circle the globe. Sailboats have been used for war, piracy, carrying cargo and passengers, fishing, racing, and just for fun.

In 1898, retired American sea captain Joshua Slocum became the first person to sail around the world by himself aboard his 37-foot-long boat, *Spray*.

WHAT ARE THEY LIKE TODAY?

Although sailing is an ancient, centuries-old art, it's one of the most popular sports in the world today. Modern sailboat racing is highly competitive, and international competitions like the Volvo Ocean Race (formerly The Whitbread) and the America's Cup push the limits of crew endurance and boat-building technology. Space-age carbon fibers and computer design are used to make more efficient hulls and sails, and millions of dollars are spent on each new boat.

But a great thing about sailboats is you don't have to be wealthy to own one. All you need is a dinghy and a sail, or a toy boat and a pond, to have your own grand adventure.

SAILBOAT ASSEMBLY

About four hours
Glue required
Models on pages 99–106

Diagram A

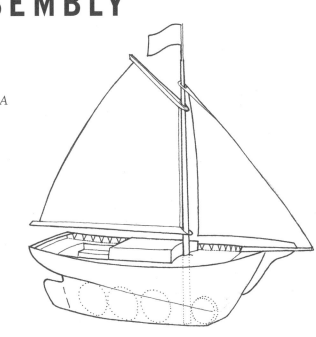

STEP 1: SCORING AND CUTTING

Score and cut out all the parts of
the sailboat.

STEP 2: HULL

Fold the hull (Part 1) where indicated
on the back of the page. Apply glue to
the lower tabs, on the area indicated by
a yellow spot, and to the inside of the
bowsprit, on the area marked by a blue
spot. Now fold the two halves of the
hull together. The lower tabs fold
inward and the pointed bowsprit sticks
out. (See Diagram A.) The rudder halves
should be glued together, but the center
section of the keel should not be, as you
will be placing the ballast there in Step
4. Look at the general diagram again;
this shows where the ballast will be.

STEP 3: TRANSOM

Fold the tabs where indicated on the
transom, or stern (Part 2), and glue in
place at the back of the hull. Make sure
you make a good joining at the base of
the stern. It will help if you can hold
the parts together with a paper clip, as
indicated on Diagram B. You can also
see the position of the tabs on this diagram (only one side shown). Note that
the tabs are inside the hull.

STEP 4: BALLAST

You will need three quarters and two
nickels for the ballast, though anything
of similar weight and size will do. Put a
spot of glue on each side of the quarters
and insert into the slot inside the keel
(Part 1) where indicated on Diagram A.
Now stick the two nickels together and
insert them into the front of the keel.
Finally, glue the green hull reinforcement
piece into the hull where indicated by
the green rectangle on the inside of
the hull. Set the whole hull assembly
aside to dry.

Diagram B

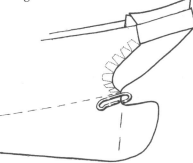

STEP 5: DECK AND DECKHOUSE ASSEMBLY

Note that there is an area on the deck
(Part 3) indicated by a red shading that
should be cut out and discarded.
Crease the deck and deckhouse (Part
4) along the scored lines, paying particular attention to the direction of the
folds as indicated by the dotted or
dashed lines. Note that the deckhouse
has some curved folds. These should
first be creased, and then folded by
pinching between your finger and thumb,
going carefully along the fold in small
movements. Study Diagram C, which
shows the shape of the complete deckhouse. Form into shape and glue the tabs,
following the system of color, matching
the spots as you go. Now stick the deckhouse onto the deck. This is stuck on
from underneath, sticking first the roof
at the front (red spot), followed by the
side tabs and finally the three tabs at
the back (pink and purple spots).

STEP 6: FLOAT-TESTING

Before you stick the deck onto the hull, you must test for leaks. Float-test your hull for a few minutes. If your hull fills with water but you can't see where it is coming in, follow this procedure: Take the hull out of the water and empty it. Carefully dry the outside, then fill the hull with water. You should now be able to see where the water is escaping. Seal up any leaks by running a bit of glue down the inside of the hull (dry it first). Allow a good bit of time for the glue to dry, and then float-test again.

STEP 7: FIXING DECK TO HULL

If you are going to color the edges of the deck, do it now. Fold all the tabs where indicated on the deck. Start gluing the deck in place, beginning at the stern. The deck fits inside the hull, and the tabs at the edge of the deck should be level with the top edge of the hull. See Diagram A. Work slowly and carefully, gluing an inch or two at a time, fix one side first, then the other. Finally, glue down the triangular bow section.

Diagram C

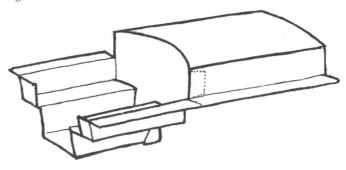

STEP 8: MAST AND BOWSPRIT

Diagram D

Crease the mast (Part 5) and bowsprit (Part 6). These parts are triangular in section (see Diagram D) and will end up looking like triangular tubes. Glue with the colored area outside. When dry, the mast can be joined to the hull. Put a little glue on the bottom (thicker) end of the mast and insert into the hole in the deck just in front of the deckhouse. Note in Diagram A that the back of the mast is flat. Push in until the mast reaches the keel, then gently crush the end of the mast, so that it may pass into the middle of the keel. Diagram A shows the mast below the deck with dotted lines. Now glue the bowsprit; the position of this piece is shown in Diagram A.

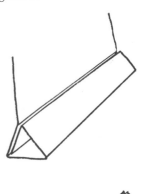

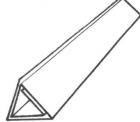

STEP 9: SAILS

Fold the mainsail (Part 7). Note that one of the fold lines (on the bottom of the mainsail) is shown as a white dotted line. The top and bottom are triangular, to form the necessary spars (see Diagram D). These fold and stick in the same way as the mast, but one fold goes backward. When dry, carefully thread over the mast. Now fold the foresail (Part 8). (The foresail has a small foldline at the top. This is shown as a dotted line.) Fold over the section at the top and thread onto the mast. Glue the bottom of the foresail to the bowsprit. Finally, take the flag (Part 9), and push it into the top of the mast.

During the American Civil War (1861–1865), coastal cities in the Confederate South needed food and their armies needed supplies, but the North's Union Navy had placed blockades of dozens of large wooden warships across the mouths of the bays and rivers of southern cities. The Confederates needed to break through these lines of ships. To do this, they built ships covered with thick iron armor that could attack the Union's fleet.

WHAT'S THEIR HISTORY?

Although most warships at this time had both steam engines and sails, they were still made of wood and looked the same as they did a hundred years before. The *Merrimack* started out as a wooden ship, too. The Confederates used the *Merrimack*'s hull and built it into an armored ship. Here's how it happened.

The *Merrimack* had once been a Union steam-powered warship, but the Union Navy abandoned it when their base at Norfolk, Virginia, was captured by the Confederates. The Confederate Navy built a new deck and sloping sides on the *Merrimack* out of wood that was two feet thick and covered with four inches of iron plate. The new *Merrimack* was 275 feet long, had a crew of 200, and 12 large guns. It was so heavy with its armor that its deck was nearly level with the water. Although the Confederate Navy renamed the

THE MONITOR & THE MERRIMACK

Merrimack the CSS *Virginia*, historians still remember it by its original name.

At the same time, the Union Navy in the North was making armored ships of its own. The first to be completed was the *Monitor*. It was 172 feet long and had a flat deck made of hardwood covered with two-inch-thick plates of iron. On the deck was a single round turret, a protective covering for the ship's two large guns, armored with plates of iron and 20 feet across. The giant turret could turn to point its guns in any direction. It was the first ship in history able to do this.

THE BATTLE OF HAMPTON ROADS

On March 8th, 1862, the Confederate ship *Merrimack* steamed out into Hampton Roads to attack the Union blockade fleet that was stopping the Confederates from bringing food and supplies to Norfolk. Although the Union Navy's powerful ships blasted away with all their guns, the shells bounced off the *Merrimack*'s armored sides. Two of the Union's best ships were sunk and another was badly damaged before the *Merrimack*'s captain chose to take his ship back under the protection of the Confederate shore guns for the night.

The Union Navy's new ship, the *Monitor*, arrived during the night to protect the blockading fleet. Early the next morning, when the *Merrimack* came out to finish off the Union ship it had crippled the day before, the *Monitor* was there to challenge it. The two armored ships fought each other for nearly four hours.

Although the *Merrimack* was larger than the *Monitor*, the ironclads were evenly matched, and neither ship could defeat the other or claim victory in this great battle.

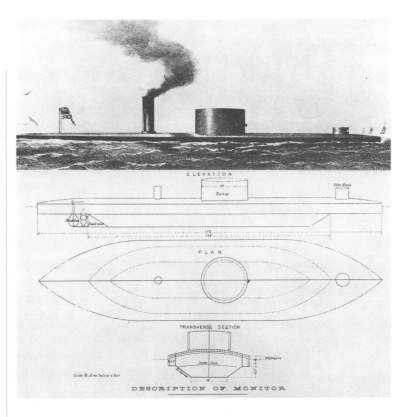

ELEVATION

PLAN

TRANSVERSE SECTION

DESCRIPTION OF MONITOR

However, the *Monitor* was able to keep the *Merrimack* from breaking the Union blockade.

What happened to the *Merrimack* and the *Monitor*? Months later, when the Union army captured Norfolk, the Confederates burned the *Merrimack* to keep it from being captured. The *Monitor* was lost at sea later that year as it was being towed to a new battle.

WHY WAS THIS BATTLE IMPORTANT?

When the Union Navy's ship *Monitor* and the Confederate Navy's *Merrimack* fought in 1862, it was the first time in history that two ships armored with iron met in combat at sea.

These two ships were the first of many ironclad warships used by both sides during the Civil War. The age of wooden warships was over. Soon, larger armored ships would be built and the era of the modern battleship would begin.

MONITOR ASSEMBLY

About two hours
Glue required
Model on pages 107–108

This boat is very easy to make, but it is important to assemble it as carefully as possible so that you can best see its curious shape.

STEP 1: SCORING AND CUTTING

Score and cut out all the parts of the *Monitor*.

STEP 2: UNDER-HULL

Fold the under-hull (Part 1) as indicated by crease lines. Study Diagram A, which shows the hull and under-hull assembly upside down, to understand the shape. Stick the small, triangular gusset area at each end of the under-hull. Now stick the under-hull in position on the bottom of the main hull (Part 2), where indicated by the thin black line. The under-hull is not supposed to be waterproof on the model, so you do not have to worry about making perfectly sealed joints on this part.

Diagram A

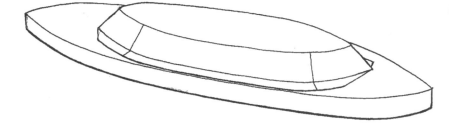

STEP 3: MAIN HULL ASSEMBLY

Fold all tabs on the main hull (Part 2), making extra sharp creases on the triangular tabs along the hull sides (the long thin strips). Apply glue to the end tabs of one strip (marked with a red spot) and join the side strips, bringing the red spots together, and forming a point. Next, apply glue to the tabs along the hull bottom and fix to the sides, forming the end of the hull. Repeat at the other end. Now examine the inside of the hull carefully for any holes. Apply glue to seal any leaks. It is important to make sure that the main hull is waterproof before you fix the deck.

STEP 4: DECK

Apply glue to the long center tab and stick down. Look along the hull from one end and make sure it isn't twisted; it will still be possible to straighten it by adjusting the position of the deck before the glue is fully dried. Next, glue the ends. You can apply glue by carefully bending up the deck at each end. Position the ends carefully, making sure that the top joining between hull and deck is as neat as possible.

Diagram B

STEP 5: GUN TURRET

Fold in the many tabs on the turret strip (Part 3), and stick the two ends, bringing the green spots together and forming a cylinder. When dry, apply glue to the bottom tabs and stick on the base (Part 4). The gun openings in the turret are nearer the bottom; the base of the turret is the O-shaped part with a hole in it. Check the joint and make sure it's as neat as possible. Now it's time to fit the retainer ring (Part 5). This part allows the turret to rotate. A rotating gun turret was a new invention used for the first time on the *Monitor*. Study Diagram B, and fold up the flaps on the edge of the tabs just a little, as shown in the diagram. Next, carefully fold up the pale blue flaps, just enough to push them into the hole in the base of the turret. Once in the hole, the flaps should spring outward, holding the retainer ring in place. Check that the retainer ring can turn.

STEP 6: TURRET FINISHING

Stick the top of the turret (Part 6) onto the rest of the turret. Do this carefully, making sure that the joint is as neat as possible. Finally, fix the completed turret in place on the pale circle on the deck. Apply glue to the yellow spots on the retainer ring, and make sure you don't get glue anywhere else or the turret may not revolve.

STEP 7: PILOTHOUSE, FLAGS

Fold the pilothouse (Part 7) to form a little box (see Diagram C). When dry, glue onto the deck where indicated by the pale gray rectangle. Fold both flagpole assemblies (Parts 8A and 8B). Note that the fold lines (and one small cut) are indicated in white on these parts. Finally, glue the two flagpoles in place where shown on Diagram C.

Diagram C

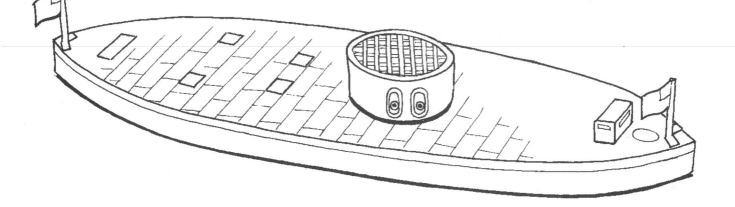

MERRIMACK ASSEMBLY

About four hours
Glue required
Model on pages 109–112

This model is constructed to the same scale as the *Monitor* model. You will notice that the *Merrimack* is much larger, however. The two ships were evenly matched in combat, because the *Monitor* had a rotating gun turret and was therefore able to fire from any angle.

STEP 1: SCORING AND CUTTING

Score and cut out all the parts of the *Merrimack*. Note that the widely spaced dashed lines inside the hull (Part 1) are curve lines and should not be scored.

STEP 2: FRONT OF HULL

Examine the front section of the hull (Part 1). Note Diagram A, which shows that the sides of the hull need to be curved. Make the curves by curving the sides around a pencil where the curve line is indicated by a widely spaced dashed line inside the hull. Fold down the rear flap of the deck section (bringing the yellow spots together) and glue, forming a 90-degree angle. Next, glue the bow together, then glue the front deck in place, with the tabs inside the hull. Now glue the front section of the hull to the sides. The edges overlap more at the top of the sides. Apply glue to the inside of the hull sides where marked by the blue-shaded area; fold up so that the overlap is formed. Now apply glue to the top side tabs; fold over, bringing the green spots together. Make sure that the hull sides are parallel.

STEP 3: REAR OF HULL

Cut the lower rear hull (Part 2). Note that the propeller can also be cut out for greater detail, if desired. Fold the hull, gluing the rear tabs inside to hold the stern together. Stick the two top flaps together. Fold the tabs inward on the rear deck (Part 3) and stick on top of the lower hull. Check underneath to make sure that the white area is covered. When dry, apply glue to the inside of the front hull on the red-shaded area, and join the two halves of the hull together. Glue down the bottom tab first, then the two sides. Check the outside to make sure that there are no white areas showing, and make sure that the hull is straight. Finally, stick in the two top tabs.

Diagram A

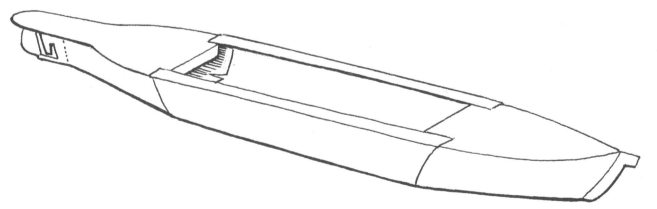

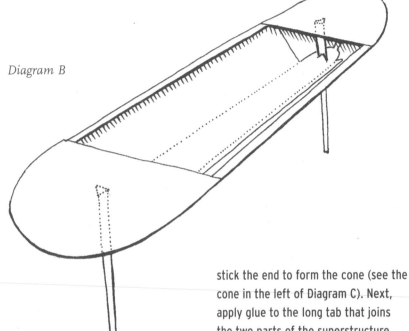

Diagram B

STEP 4: SUPERSTRUCTURE

See Diagram B, which shows the super-structure assembly upside down. Fold the two main parts (Parts 4 and 5). Take the part with the small red spot and curve the round end until the two red spots meet. Glue together, forming one side and one end of the superstructure. Now fold the other half of the super-structure; this is the same except there is a small cone-shaped structure (the pilot turret) at one end. This is circular at first, but the edges should be over-lapped, pulling them until the structure becomes cone-shaped (this also curves the end of the superstructure). When you have formed the shape, apply glue to the red-shaded area and pull in and

stick the end to form the cone (see the cone in the left of Diagram C). Next, apply glue to the long tab that joins the two parts of the superstructure, followed by the tabs that join the ends.

STEP 5: REINFORCEMENT

Stick the two semicircular reinforcement panels (Parts 6 and 7) to the bottom of the superstructure where indicated on Diagram B. Start at the center of each panel (line up the green spots) and work outward. The edge of the superstructure should just overlap, so that you can't see the panel when you look from above. Next, the two masts (Parts 8A and 8B) should be creased very sharply using a straight edge, then glued, making trian-gular tubes. They should then be glued in place, pushing through their holes in the superstructure, and stuck down on the semicircular reinforcement panels below. See Diagrams B and C.

STEP 6: BALLAST

If you are going to float your model, you will need to make it watertight. Check that there are no visible holes in the hull. If you find any, stop them up with a little glue applied from inside. To make your model float straight you will need to add a couple of small weights, one at each end. Test in the water and check that the hull floats straight. Alternatively, you may decide to make your model float so that the water line is at the correct height (which is harder). One of the most unusual features of the *Merrimack* was the position of the water line, which is indicated by the top of the brown parts. The gray area of the superstructure (the iron-plate armor) was the only part that showed above the water. To achieve this effect you will have to waterproof your hull very well, and add a great deal of bal-last to make your model float at the correct level.

STEP 7: FIXING SUPERSTRUCTURE

Apply glue to the bottom of the super-structure and fix onto the hull where indicated by the thin black lines. It may help to form a strong joining if you pinch along the sides of the seam using your finger and thumb, but take care not to crush the model.

STEP 8: BOW BULWARK

Fold the bow bulwark (Part 9). The fold lines are shown in white on this V-shaped part. Glue to the front deck as shown in Diagram C.

STEP 9: SMOKESTACK

Roll the smokestack (Part 10) around a pencil. Apply glue to the overlap area and fix. When the overlap area is dry, apply glue to the inside of the long strip and roll around the smokestack. Fold in the tabs at the base, and stick in place on the superstructure. Note that the seam is at the back and the smokestack leans slightly backward.

STEP 10: SHIP'S BOATS

Fold the ship's boats (Parts 11A and 11B). Note that the fold lines are on a brown background. First join the keel section (the small V-shaped section in the middle). When dry, test-fold the stern section, forming the transom and seat. Careful bending is required here. When you are satisfied, apply glue to the tabs and fix. Next, fix the bow tab, then the two seats. Check that the boat is straight and even before the glue sets completely. Repeat for the second boat. Fold the ends of the two boat supports (Parts 12A and 12B) up at 90 degrees. Test-fit your boats on the supports to get the position right. When you are ready, apply a tiny bit of glue to the cutout at each end, and then fix the boat in place. Next, fix the two boat-and-support assemblies in place on the side of the superstructure, where indicated by the thin black lines. Use Diagram C as your guide.

STEP 11: VENTILATORS, FLAGS

Fold the ventilators (Parts 13A and 13B) in half. Note that the bottom of each side folds out. Glue in place on the superstructure on each side of the smokestack. See Diagram C. Finally, cut out the two Confederate flags (Parts 14A and 14B) and glue into place on the masts.

Diagram C

AIRCRAFT CARRIER

Modern aircraft carriers are the most powerful and important vessels in the U.S. Navy. Carriers are floating military bases that can be placed anywhere on the oceans of the world, wherever they are needed to keep the peace. These huge and fast ships are floating cities, equipped with everything needed by their crews of over 5,000. They can carry dozens of airplanes and helicopters, as well as cruise missiles, which can extend the carriers' reach hundreds of miles inland.

WHAT'S THEIR HISTORY?

The first experiments with using airplanes on ships began in 1910. Large wooden decks were added to ships for the planes to take off and land. The U.S. Navy's first aircraft carrier, the USS *Langley*, was commissioned in 1922.

Before World War II (1939–1945), battleships with huge guns were the most powerful ships in the world's navies. But during the war, aircraft carriers proved that naval air power was the wave of the future.

Take, for example, the USS *Intrepid*, one of 24 fast-attack Essex-Class carriers built by the U.S. Navy. The *Intrepid* was huge and one of the fastest warships in the world. Launched in 1943, the *Intrepid* took part in the largest naval battle in history, the Battle of Leyte Gulf. It was also hit by a torpedo and four Japanese kamikaze suicide planes, which killed dozens of the crew and nearly sank the ship. But the *Intrepid* survived these attacks. Each time it was damaged the carrier was quickly repaired and put back into service. The Japanese were so surprised to see the *Intrepid* reappear that they called it "The Ghost Ship."

After the war, the *Intrepid* was modernized with a new angled deck to carry jet aircraft. In the early 1960s, the *Intrepid* served as a prime recovery vessel for NASA. Its job was to pick up Mercury and Gemini astronauts and their spacecraft after they parachuted to Earth from space. The *Intrepid* also served three tours of duty during the Vietnam War and ended its military career in 1974 tracking Soviet submarines in the Atlantic Ocean during the Cold War.

The USS *Intrepid* is now the popular Intrepid Sea Air Space Museum in New York City. From warship to museum, the USS *Intrepid* continues its voyage through history as one of the greatest aircraft carriers ever built.

WHAT ARE AIRCRAFT CARRIERS LIKE TODAY?

Today's carriers can weigh over 80,000 tons and are over 1,000 feet long. They speed through the sea at 30 knots. Supercarriers are powered by nuclear reactors. This type of power makes them capable of cruising non-stop for 20 years—without being refueled!

AIRCRAFT CARRIER ASSEMBLY

About two to three hours
Glue required
Model on pages 113–116

STEP 1: SCORING AND CUTTING

Score and cut out all the parts. Note that the widely spaced dashed lines inside the hull indicate curves and should not be scored.

STEP 2: HULL, BOW SECTION

See Diagram A. Fold the bow section (Part 1). This model has some fold lines that should be formed as curves instead of sharp creases; these are indicated by widely spaced dashed lines. These curves should be formed around a pencil or something similar. You will notice a small gray area on the back of the sheet. This area should be cut around three sides and folded out. (See Diagram A.) Stick lower bow tab first (indicated by a red spot). When dry, stick upper bow area. This part is not pointed, but forms a flat triangular area. Apply glue to the white area on the outside of the bow and fix, bringing the green spots together. The colored areas should exactly meet up, hiding the white-tab area. Finally, stick the two top tabs together.

Diagram A

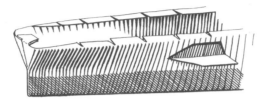

STEP 3: CENTER HULL, STERN

Fold the central hull and stern (Part 2), forming tight creases at the gussets (these are the small triangular areas, one on each side and one at the stern). Apply glue to one of the side gussets and top tab. Fold the gusset in and pull tight by pulling the parts of the top tab together where they overlap. Make sure that the top tab forms a straight line. When dry, repeat for the other side, then stick the stern gusset in the same way. When you have stuck the stern, fix the two top tabs together so that they line up exactly.

STEP 4: FIXING HULL HALVES

Apply glue to the white areas on the outside of the bow section, and stick the two halves together. Make sure that the white areas are covered; the edges of the colored area should meet up exactly. The center lines (marked in red on the inside of each part) should also meet. Allow to dry thoroughly, then stick the top tabs together on each side, making sure that the top tab forms a straight line on each side.

Diagram B

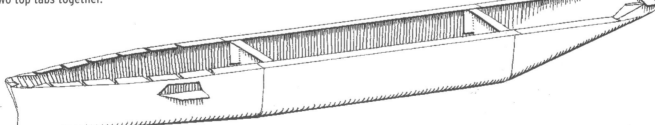

STEP 5: BULKHEADS

See Diagram B. Fold the two bulkheads (Parts 3 and 4). Now stick the top and side tabs together on each bulkhead, bringing the green spots together. When dry, fix inside the hull as shown in Diagram B. One bulkhead is fixed against the gusset at the stern, the other on top of the overlap area where the hull is fixed together. When you fix the bulkheads, make sure you push them down and that the top tab will fold down on top of the bulkhead at each side. When dry, the top tab can be stuck down on the bulkhead. Your hull should resemble Diagram B.

STEP 6: FLOAT-TESTING

You can now float-test your hull. Check for any leaks, especially at the joining. If water gets in, apply glue to the inside of the hull, and retest when dry. To make your model float more realistically, add a small weight (a couple of coins, a small pebble, or modeling clay) to each end of the hull. Make sure that the hull floats straight, though you may have to retest and add a tiny weight to adjust the trim (the way the vessel floats in the water) when the model is finished. This can be glued to the underside of the flight deck opposite the superstructure.

STEP 7: DECK

Glue the yellow tabs on the two deck pieces (Parts 5 and 6). Put glue on the tabs of the hull and join the deck to the hull.

STEP 8: SUPERSTRUCTURE

See Diagrams C and D. The superstructure (Part 7) looks complex, but with careful cutting and folding the assembly is really quite easy: nearly all the structure is made up of simple box shapes. (Be sure to make the short cut indicated by a red arrow on the back of the sheet.) It is important that you follow the correct assembly sequence, explained below. Before you start, study Diagram C which shows the cutting and folding of the mast. This is perhaps the hardest part, and if it looks too tricky the upper (pointed) part of the mast need not be cut. Your model will still look great.

Diagram C

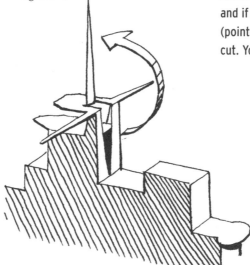

Fold all the creases. These are 90-degree folds. Stick the tabs with green spots in place, forming a small open box at each end of the structure. Next, stick the yellow-spot tabs, tucking them into the tops of the little boxes you have already made, forming the outer guns. Next, stick the orange-spot tabs, forming a taller box at each end. The tabs with red spots are next.

Diagram D

They form the inner guns and the top of the additional box. Next, the main part of the superstructure is formed by gluing the violet tabs. This will be easier if you fold back the "lids" of the various parts, but check that you have lined up the tabs properly by trial-folding in the lids to make sure they'll fit. Don't fix the lids yet. There is one more side tab at the side of the smokestack/mast assembly (marked with a blue spot) that passes through the little slot mentioned earlier, indicated by the red arrow. See Diagram C for the final shape you're aiming for.

Now glue the blue-spot tab and fix down all the lid flaps. You can now glue the superstructure island in place on the deck where indicated by the plain brown rectangle. Also see Diagram D.

PT BOAT

To be a crew member of a PT boat, you have to be daring and brave. Your job: to attack enemy vessels using torpedoes launched from tubes on your boat's deck. These high-speed, powerful little patrol boats were made of wood and powered by four aircraft engines. Their crews included two officers and nine enlisted men.

WHAT'S THEIR HISTORY?

Patrol Torpedo (PT) boats were first developed in the late 1800s. The idea was that small, fast boats could attack and sink large warships. Torpedo boats were used in 1898 in the Spanish American War and again in World War I (1914–1918). But it was during World War II that PT boats became famous.

The United States produced nearly 800 PTs, which were made by several boat-building companies in versions ranging from 75 to 80 feet long. A PT boat carried four torpedoes and depth charges (underwater bombs) to attack other ships and submarines. These boats also had machine guns and machine cannons that were used to defend themselves against

aircraft. These deck guns could also be used for close combat with surface vessels.

HOW WERE THEY USED IN WORLD WAR II?

Although PT Boats were used all over the world by the U.S. Navy and several allies, they are best known for their service in the South Pacific against the Japanese during World War II. PT boat squadrons operated from small island bases. From these forward positions, they attacked enemy warships, troop transports, and supply ships.

PT boats often carried out hit-and-run attacks under the cover of darkness. During daylight missions, they could lay down thick smoke screens produced by smoke generators carried on their decks. The Japanese called them "mosquito boats" because they were small, fast, hard to hit, and delivered a painful sting!

Although they were made of wood, PT boats often survived direct hits from enemy guns because small artillery shells passed in through one side and right out through the other without exploding. This is because the boats were made out of light plywood that would not give enough resistance to an artillery shell to cause it to explode. They also had such a shallow draft (depth under the water) that enemy torpedoes passed right underneath them.

JOHN F. KENNEDY AND *PT 109*

The best-known PT boat was *PT 109* commanded by young ensign John F. Kennedy. While on a night patrol in Japanese-held waters in 1943, *PT 109* was rammed by a Japanese destroyer and cut in half. Kennedy and most of his crew survived the collision and clung to the wreckage through the night. In the morning, they swam to a small island. Several days later, friendly natives helped them make contact with an Australian coast-watcher who arranged for another PT boat to rescue them. Kennedy went on to become America's 35th president in 1961.

PT BOAT ASSEMBLY

About three hours
Glue optional
Model on pages 117–118

This boat can be assembled without glue, but if you decide to use glue for assembly there are notes in the instructions that tell you what to do as you go along.

Diagram A

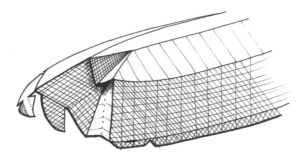

STEP 1: SCORING AND CUTTING

Score and cut out all the pieces. If using glue, do not cut out the nine slits on each side of the hull (Part 1), but do cut the slit marked by an orange spot at the bow. Instead, make six small V-shaped cuts indicated in green on the back (plan) side of the page. Also, the nine petal-shaped tabs on either side of the deck (Part 3) should be cut off.

If you are not using glue, cut out all the parts and make all the slits indicated, however, do not make the six small V-shaped cuts indicated in green on Part 1.

STEP 2: HULL

Crease and fold the hull (Part 1) where indicated. Start folding the bow section as shown in Diagram A. The small kite-shaped area folds inward, bringing the green spots together. Squeeze the bow to form a good sharp point. If using glue, apply a little to the inside of the bow fold to hold its two halves together. Inside the bow there is a triangular pocket. Fold this in half, bringing the yellow spots together. Next, fold the flap of the orange-spot tab to form a small deck area at the bow. Now fold in the flap of the orange-spot tab and insert into the orange-spot slot to secure. The flap on this tab may not open by itself, in which case you should ease it open with a pointed instrument.

STEP 3: STERN

Fold in the corners of the stern, bringing the red spots together. These areas may be glued if you wish. You will now have a triangular pocket inside the hull. (See Diagram B, left side.) Now fold down one of the long rectangular tabs, bringing the yellow spots together. Finally, the blue triangular flap folds underneath the pocket, holding the stern together. (See the right side of Diagram B.)

Diagram B

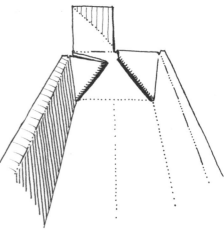

Diagram C

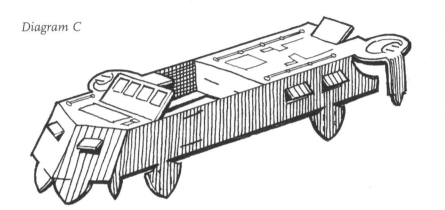

STEP 4: SUPERSTRUCTURE, DECK

Fold the superstructure and deck (Parts 2 and 3), as shown in Diagrams C and D. (Make sure you cut all the little slots where indicated on the plan side of these parts. There are two small areas that you should cut out and discard, and these are indicated by red shading on the plan.) Next, start fitting the superstructure to the deck. Begin by fixing the two red-spot tabs at the front of the superstructure. These tabs and all the others securing the super-structure are easier to insert if you open their slots a little with a pointed object and pull them through from below. All other tabs fit into their slots. The process is easier if you start several tabs at once and ease them into their slots a little at a time, pulling from below.

STEP 5: TORPEDO TUBES

Shape the four torpedo tubes (Parts 4A, 4B, 4C, and 4D) by rolling each piece around a thin pencil or paintbrush. The tabs pass through the slots in each tube, then through the matching slots in the deck to fix them in place. The torpedo tubes are marked with colored spots, red for port (4A and 4B) and green for starboard (4C and 4D), so you'll know on which side to fit them.

STEP 6: FIXING DECK TO HULL

For both types of assembly, fold in the flaps of the green-spot tab on the front of the deck. Now turn the deck upside down and insert the tab into its matching slot on the front of the hull. Unfold the locking flaps, and then fold

the deck back into position. If you are using glue, apply it to the side tabs on the top of the hull one side at a time, and fix carefully into position, taking care to form a neat joint along the top edge of the hull. If you are using the no-glue method, proceed as follows: Study Diagram D. Now pull backward and up on the deck, curving it upward as shown in the diagram. This will enable you to insert the first yellow-spot leaf tab into the corresponding spot on the hull. As you feed the tab into its slot, lower the deck carefully into position. Repeat on the other side. Now work toward the stern, inserting the tabs in turn until you reach the blue-spot tab, which locks the deck into position. As you fix the deck, you may find it necessary to twist and turn the deck and hull to make it easier to insert the tabs. When you have finished, pinch along the joint between the deck and hull to straighten it and reduce any bumps or bulges.

Diagram D

STEP 7: MAST

Note the three small areas on the mast (Part 5) that you should cut out and discard. Fold the mast as shown on the Diagram E. Open the two slits on the superstructure to form "pockets" and insert the two front tabs of the mast. Now widen the slot on the superstructure roof, insert the rear support of the mast, and adjust the assembled mast to resemble the diagram.

STEP 8: ANTIAIRCRAFT GUNS

You can omit the antiaircraft guns (Parts 6A and 6B) from your model if you prefer. Alternatively, for a super-detailed appearance, you can cut out the white area between the gun barrels. To assemble, fold the guns. Note that the top fold lines are shown as white dotted lines on black. Widen the two slots on each turret of the superstructure (see Diagram E) and fix the guns in place on their turrets. It's easiest to unfold the gun temporarily, fix one of the tabs in the turret, then refold and insert the second tab.

STEP 9: MAIN DECK GUN

Fold the main deck gun (Part 7). Note the two small cutout parts that stand up when the gun is folded into shape. (See Diagram E.) Next, open the mounting slots and fix the gun in place. Fold the flag (Part 8), and fix the central slot at the stern. Finally, fix the radio mast (Part 9) into the twin slots on the side of the superstructure.

Diagram E

Tugboats are tough workboats. There are probably more shapes and sizes of tugboats than of any other kind of vessel. Some are designed and built to do very specific kinds of work, while others can do almost anything.

WHAT'S THEIR HISTORY?

Tugs were first developed in the early 1800s, soon after the introduction of steam engines. The most important task of early tugboats was to tow huge sailing ships in and out of crowded harbors. Before tugboats, sailing ships had to wait for just the right wind and tide conditions to begin or end their voyages. The other important task tugs have always

done is moving barges. Barges are basically large hulls that carry cargo and have no power of their own. Tugboats are like floating tow trucks or train engines, and barges are like the trailers, or freight cars, of the sea.

The first tugs were made of wood and used side paddle wheels for power. By the mid-1800s, however, tugs used propellers and began to look like they do now.

HOW DO THEY WORK?

There are three ways tugs move things. "Pushing ahead" is when tugs push with their rounded noses, which are padded with large rubber fenders. "Towing astern" is when tugs use long heavy ropes or wire cables called hawsers to pull a ship or a barge.

TUGBOAT

Towing "on the hip" is when tugs tie up alongside a ship or a barge to help move them forward or back. Old tires hang from the sides of tugs to act as fenders when they are towing on the hip.

There are basically three kinds of tugs. Harbor tugs are used to push and pull barges, and help nudge large ships into and out of their docking slips. Coastal tugs push or tow large barges long distances. Some tugs are designed to fit into notches in specially made barges. They are locked together and become ships called "integrated units." The largest tugboats are ocean-going tugs, often called salvage tugs. These tugs are huge and power-ful and can move giant barges across oceans. They are also used to rescue large ships that have lost power at sea. Salvage tugs carry large crews and can help fight fires, pump water from damaged ships, and tow them to safety under almost any conditions anywhere in the world.

WHAT ARE THEY LIKE TODAY?

Today's tugs are powered by modern diesel engines. Small tugs may have only 400 horse-power while giant, monster tugs may have 6,000 or more horsepower.

Tugs are so strong and well made that many of them that were built fifty years ago or more are still working alongside the modern high-tech tugs built today. Large or small, old or new, tugboats keep the maritime world on the move.

TUGBOAT ASSEMBLY

About five hours
Glue required
Model on pages 119–120

STEP 1: SCORING AND CUTTING

Score and cut out all the pieces
of the tug.

STEP 2: HULL

Cut and fold the hull (Part 1). See
Diagram A. Fold in the four gussets
(two on each side) and stick. Each
gusset has a tab at the top. This
should be glued to the inside of the
hull; pulling the tab tight helps to hold
the gusset tightly closed while the
glue dries. Now glue the bow. Fold in
the white area, bringing the two green
spots together and holding the two
halves of the hull together, then glue.
The two small rectangular tabs at
the top should also be glued, bringing
the yellow spots together.

STEP 3: BULKHEADS, STERN

See Diagram A. Fold the two bulkheads
(Parts 2A and 2B), put glue on the tabs,
and fix them inside the hull. Test-fit the
rudder assembly (Part 3) in the slot in
the stern of the tug. Now apply some
glue to both sides of the slot and fix
the rudder, also bringing the two halves
of the stern together. It helps to clamp
this part until the glue is dry. Now glue
the two halves of the stern rail, bringing the blue spots together (the last
two tabs on each side overlap.) When
dry, stick the stern rail down onto the

top of the stern, securing by the small
tabs underneath.

STEP 4: DECK, DECKHOUSE

Apply glue to the inside of the flap
that joins the hull and deck, fold the
flap down to stick, bringing the green
spots together. Don't glue the deck yet.
Fold the main deckhouse (Part 4). Stick
the tab at the back, bringing the yellow
spots together to form a box, noting
that the front of the deckhouse is
curved. When dry, fold the roof down
and stick the two long tabs, one on
each side, and the three small tabs at
the front. Note that the roof overlaps
the walls of the deckhouse all around
the sides and front. When dry, you can
glue the deckhouse where indicated on
the main deck. First apply glue to the
long tab at the other side of the deck,

then glue, bringing the orange spots
together. The tab should be inside the
hull, so that their top edges line up.
Now apply glue to the two tabs under
the deck at the bow (see the red spots)
and the two small tabs, one on each side
of the deck. The pointed end of the deck
is slipped in under the small square
center post at the bow, and glued.

STEP 5: WHEELHOUSE, LIGHTS

Fold the wheelhouse (Part 5). You will
see that it is very similar to the main
deckhouse. When dry, glue where
indicated by the black outline on the
roof of the main deckhouse. Now, fold
the navigation lights (Parts 6A and 6B),
bringing the blue spots together. The
white tab glues to the bottom of each
light, forming a small three-sided box.
When dry, fix in place on the roof
of the wheelhouse (see Diagram C).
Remember, RED=PORT=LEFT, and
GREEN=STARBOARD=RIGHT!

Diagram A

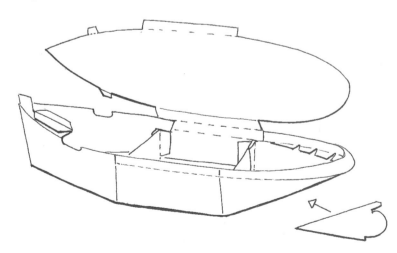

STEP 6: FUNNEL

Form the funnel (Part 7) into a cylinder by rolling it around a pencil or thin paintbrush or something similar. Apply glue to the white overlap area and stick into a cylinder. When dry, apply a little glue to the inside of the long strip and carefully glue, forming a band around the top of the funnel. You have now finished the basic assembly of your tug, but there are several more parts on the sheet to make an even more splendid model.

STEP 7: FUNNEL HOOD

Glue the white overlap area of the funnel weather hood (Part 8), bringing the red spots together to form a cone shape. When dry, do a trial fitting on the funnel. The hood slides on from below, and the tabs line up with the bottom of the funnel. Line the seams up at the back, then fix. Now fix the funnel in position, seam at the back, sloping slightly toward the rear.

STEP 8: MAST

Fold the mast (Part 9), using a straight edge or ruler to form straight, accurate creases. Now fold and glue into a triangular section tube, tapering toward the top. Note that there are five small square navigation lights projecting from the front of the mast. When the mast is dry, stick in place on the front of the deckhouse assembly with the projection lights facing forward (see Diagram C).

Diagram B

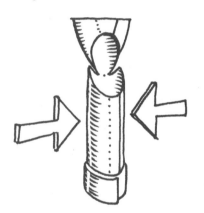

STEP 9: VENTILATORS

There are two ventilators (Parts 10A and 10B). Form into a cylinder, including the curved top section. Now stick the cylindrical section into a tube, gluing the white overlap area. When dry, glue the long strip that fits around the base (this is similar to the funnel assembly). Glue the top section of the ventilator, apply glue to the small white overlap area, the top section forming a conical shape. See Diagram B, which shows the assembly at this stage. When dry, fold the top section over the tubular base and secure with a spot of glue. The ventilator should be slightly squashed as indicated by the arrows in Diagram B, making it oval. When dry, repeat for the second ventilator, and glue the ventilators in place on the upper deck where indicated by the black circles (see Diagram C).

STEP 10: SHIP'S BOAT

This is very similar to the two boats on the deck of the *Merrimack* and is a miniature version of the rowboat model.

Fold the ship's boat (Part 11) where indicated. Glue the small keel at the stern, pinching and bringing the green spots together. Hold together as the glue dries. Next, glue the tab at the bow, followed by the seat/transom assembly. Finally, glue the seats. Check the boat from above to ensure that it is straight. Now fold the boat support (Part 12); the ends should be folded to a right angle. Glue boat support to the bottom of the boat, and finally glue the boat assembly in place on the upper deck (see Diagram C). Note that the boat support slightly overhangs the edge of the deck.

STEP 11: POSTS

There are six of these (Parts 13). Roll and glue, including the long strip around the base of each post. When the posts are dry, glue the disk on the top of each post. The complete assemblies should now be glued in place on the deck, on the black oval areas, with one post at each end. See Diagram C. These parts are small and if you find that they turn out a bit scruffy, you can touch them up with a black waterproof marker, which improves the look a great deal.

Diagram C

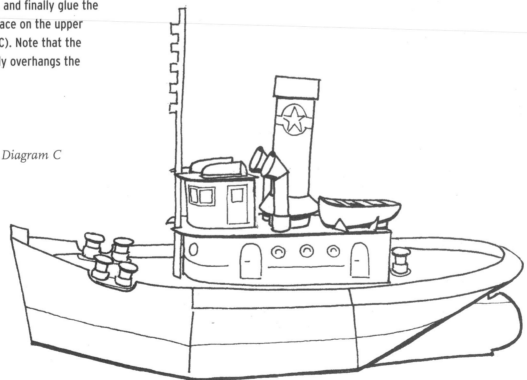

OCEAN LINER

Two hundred years ago, long before airplanes were invented, the only way to cross the Atlantic Ocean from Europe to America was aboard slow sailing ships. By the mid-1800s however, steam-powered ships were beginning to cross the Atlantic regularly. Soon, more and larger passenger ships were carrying people across the Atlantic. Although some were wealthy people traveling on business or for pleasure, most passengers were poor Europeans immigrating to the United States to find a better life.

By 1900, the golden age of the great ocean liners had begun. Ocean liners were like floating, luxurious cities, and were the largest moving objects made. These mighty ocean liners were known as "The Queens of the Seas," symbols of modern engineering and national pride.

WHAT'S THEIR HISTORY?

In the early 1900s, ship-making companies in both Germany and England built huge passenger ships with four smokestacks. These giant ocean liners competed to be known as the fastest, largest, and most beautiful ships ever built.

In England, companies such as Cunard and White Star built huge four-stackers like the *Mauritania*, the *Aquitania*, the *Olympic*, the *Titanic*, and the *Lusitania*. These ships competed for the Blue Riband, awarded to the ship that made the fastest round-trip from Europe to America and back. On their upper decks, rich travelers lived in luxury, while down below, thousands of passengers made the trip in cramped, no-frills quarters.

In the 1930s, newer ships like Italy's *Rex*, France's *Normandie*, and Great Britain's *Queen Mary* competed on the transatlantic run. During World War II, many ocean liners were painted gray and carried American soldiers to England.

After World War II, larger, faster ships like the *France* and the *Queen Elizabeth* set a new standard for speed and luxury. And in 1952, the SS *United States* was launched. It was the fastest ocean liner ever built. But

the days of the great ocean liners were already threatened by the growing popularity of long-distance airplane flight. By 1958, more people were crossing the Atlantic by air than by ship.

WHAT ARE THEY LIKE TODAY?

Today, Britain's *QE2* is the last of the great transatlantic ocean liners. But the age of luxury liners is far from over. Although only a few passengers still cross the Atlantic by sea, giant cruise ships now carry hundreds of thousands of people on floating vacations worldwide. As long as these giant ships still sail the seven seas, the feeling of romance and adventure of the great ocean liners lives on!

OCEAN LINER ASSEMBLY

About five hours
Glue required
Model on pages 121–122

Diagram B

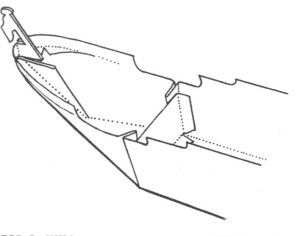

STEP 1: SCORING AND CUTTING

Score and cut out all the parts of the model. Note that the dot-dash lines on the four funnels (Parts 5) are not fold lines and should not be scored. In order to follow the lines more accurately, you will need to cut the hull (Part 1) and the deck (Part 4) from the back side of the sheet. Note that Step 8, building the lifeboats, is optional, so you don't have to cut out the four lifeboat pieces (Parts 6) unless you decide to build them. (If you decide to build the model lifeboats, trim off and discard the flat lifeboats off the side of the deck by cutting along the blue line on the back of the sheet.)

STEP 2: HULL

Fold in the four gussets on the hull (Part 1). These are the V-shaped folds, two on each side of the hull. Make sharp creases, then glue the gussets together. Take care not to get glue on the outside of the hull. Now fold in the bow, and glue. The two halves of the bow flag meet up when you fold in the bow; this area should also be glued.

STEP 3: RUDDER, BULKHEADS

Fold in the stern. Glue the rudder (Part 2) in place in the slot formed in the stern (See Diagram A). It helps to hold the stern fold and rudder tightly in place while the glue is drying. A paper clip or small binder clip is ideal for this. Now fold the bulkheads (Parts 3A and 3B). Glue the rear shorter bulkhead (Part 3A) in place as indicated in Diagram B. A paper clip on each side will help hold the bulkhead while the glue dries. Now glue the front bulkhead (Part 3B). The top of this bulkhead can be seen in Diagram A.

Diagram A

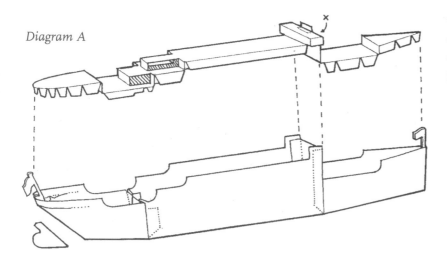

STEP 4: STERN RAIL, FLAG

Study Diagrams A and B. The flag and pole assembly at either end of the hull (Part 1) folds in as shown. The white sides come together, colored sides out. It can then be glued. When dry, the flagpole/stern rail assembly can be glued in place (held in by four small triangular tabs) to the top of the hull.

STEP 5: BALLAST

You will need two quarters (or similar weights) to ballast your hull. Glue these inside the hull, one at each end. Make sure the weights are central. You can float-test your hull at this stage to check for leaks and make sure that the hull floats straight. If there are any leaks in the hull they can be repaired by using glue on the inside.

STEP 6: DECK

Study Diagram A, which shows the shape of the deck (Part 4). There are some corner tabs on each side that should be glued to form a box at the bridge and steps in the deck, as shown in Diagram A. You can now start to attach the deck assembly. Start by gluing the bridge and front wall of the upper deck to the front bulkhead. (See "X" on Diagram A.) When this is dry, the bow section can be glued, but it's a good idea to test-fit the bow section first, before gluing. Carefully push the front part of the deck into place, making sure that the tabs are inside the hull. If all goes well, pull out and stick with glue. Repeat the process for the stern area. The test-fit is particularly important here, as you will notice that the deck has to slide into position underneath the flagpole assembly.

STEP 7: FUNNELS

The dot-dash line on the four funnels (Parts 5) is NOT a fold line, but instead it shows where the paper must overlap when you form each funnel into a cylinder. Roll each funnel around a pencil to form a smooth curve, then glue it, forming a cylinder. When dry, squash the cylinder carefully into an oval shape. The seam should be at the back, at one of the narrow ends of the oval. Now glue the first base cover (the white rounds at the base of each funnel) into place; the small tab on the first base cover pokes into the funnel and holds it in place. When dry, glue the second base cover over the first. You can now glue the funnel onto the top deck, where indicated by the gray oval shape. Repeat for the remaining three funnels. Note that all the funnels slope backward. See Diagram D for how the funnels should appear on the finished model.

Diagram C

Diagram D

STEP 8: LIFEBOATS

The lifeboats (Parts 6) are optional. Making them is tricky because they are so small, and your liner will look splendid even if you don't use them. But if you want to give it a try, your liner will be even more impressive with the three-dimensional lifeboats. Start by cutting out the four lifeboat parts (Parts 6). Now carefully score and fold the creases where indicated on the back. Each tiny lifeboat has a curved fold line; when creased, these form shallow pockets, which will become one side of each lifeboat. Look at Diagram C, which shows an assembled row of lifeboats. After all the boats are creased, the two halves of the lifeboat assembly can be glued together. The glue should be applied to the area beween the boats, taking care not to stick the actual boats themselves. When the glue is dry, the whole assembly can be straightened out. The lifeboats will then open out to their proper boat shape. Well done! You can now fix the lifeboats in place on the edge of the upper deck, beside the funnels. Repeat for the other side.

STEP 9: MASTS

Fold the masts (Parts 7A and 7B). Use a ruler or straight edge to get straight, sharp creases. The masts are triangular in section, and should be folded with the white strip inside. The front mast has a small projection that should point forward when assembled. First, perform a test-fit. Lay the mast on a flat surface, and pinch it into a triangular shape; run your forefinger and thumb up and down the mast, squeezing it into a triangular tube and keeping the creases as sharp as possible. Now apply a thin layer of glue along the inside edge of the mast and repeat the process. When the glue is dry, test-fit the mast in its triangular hole. Remove and apply glue to the end. Push in until the mast meets the bottom of the hull. Look at the liner from one end to make sure the mast is straight and not leaning to one side. The mast should lean slightly toward the back of the ship, at about the same angle as the funnels.

Long before there were roads or trains, the Mississippi River formed a natural highway down the center of America. The river allowed cargo and passengers to travel north and south between the great industrial and agricultural cities and the Gulf of Mexico. Paddle-wheel riverboats were developed to navigate the shallow waters of the Mississippi River and to fight its strong current. In fact, these were the first ships designed specifically to navigate America's shallow rivers.

WHAT'S THEIR HISTORY?

In colonial times, large log rafts carried cargo on one-way trips down the Mississippi, from north to south with the flow of the river. When the rafts reached New Orleans, the cargo was unloaded, and the raft was taken apart so the logs could be sold.

Later, small flatboats loaded with cargo were pushed with poles along the river. While going downstream, the current helped push the boat. But when returning upstream, the boats had to fight the flow of the water. It took two months to make a river trip from Pittsburgh to New Orleans, but twice as long coming back! All that changed with the introduction of steam power.

The riverboat *New Orleans*, built by Robert Fulton in 1811, was the first paddle-wheel steamship used on, but not designed for, the Mississippi. Deep-hulled vessels built

MISSISSIPPI PADDLE WHEELER

in the east for deep water use were not suitable for the shallow Mississippi River, where shifting sandbars were (and are) a constant obstacle.

The first paddle wheeler designed for the Mississippi was the *George Washington*, built in 1816. Like all true riverboats, it was built like a large flat-bottomed raft with its steam engine on deck instead of down inside the ship. A second or third level was built onto the main deck to carry passengers.

Mississippi steamboats were either "side wheelers" or "stern wheelers." Side wheelers had two paddles, one on each side, while stern wheelers had just one paddle at the back. Both designs had twin smokestacks, side by side, with fancy tops. Almost all boats were painted white. Some were built especially to carry cargo. Large "cotton packets" could carry 7,000 bales of cotton stacked like building blocks on their decks. Others were

built to carry hundreds of passengers from one city to another. These boats often featured ornate decorations, and beautiful dining rooms and sleeping cabins. Riverboats also became famous for gambling.

Perhaps the most famous paddle-wheel captain was American writer Samuel Clemens. His pseudonym, Mark Twain, was taken from a phrase used on riverboats to note the depth of the water. In his day, sounders would shout "By the mark, twain" to note a water depth of 2 fathoms, or 12 feet.

WHAT ARE THEY LIKE TODAY?

Although they were developed almost two hundred years ago, paddle-wheel riverboats are still popular today. They no longer carry cargo, but thousands of passengers enjoy sightseeing journeys up and down the mighty Mississippi aboard dozens of splendidly decorated paddle wheelers.

MISSISSIPPI PADDLE WHEELER ASSEMBLY

About seven hours
No glue required
Model on pages 123–128

To make this boat, you will also need:
• Two thin rubber bands
• Thin wire or string
• Wooden matchsticks

This model is the most complex in the book, yet it has been designed so that it may be constructed without glue. To make construction easier, take great care in cutting out the various parts. This model has the great advantage that it is self-propelled, and should be capable of completing many lengths of the bathtub, or traveling a reasonable distance on a calm pond or pool.

STEP 1: SCORING AND CUTTING
Score and cut out all the parts, making an extra effort to cut them exactly.

STEP 2: HULL
Refer to Diagram A, which shows the hull (Part 1) upside down. Fold and assemble the stern. Tuck the small black tab (marked with a red spot) into its slot (also marked with a red spot). Fold in the top flap of the wheel support and fold and insert the locking tab marked with a bright green spot into its slot, also marked. Repeat for both sides of the stern. The bow can be folded in at this stage, forming a pocket in the center, but it cannot be attached until after you attach the deck.

Diagram A

STEP 3: BALLAST
You will need some ballast to help keep the paddle wheeler level. Fix two quarters (or modeling clay or a small pebble) in place where marked by the dotted circle inside the hull.

STEP 4: DECK
Fold the main deck (Part 2). Now pull the two halves of the bow together. The two tabs marked with a yellow spot pass through the slot in the deck that is also marked with a yellow spot. It will help if you hold the pocket formed in the bow to one side while you do this. Now insert the locking tabs through their respective slots in the deck, working backward from the bow. When you reach the leaf-shaped tabs, fold in the rectangular areas in the hull sides, inserting the tabs as you go, working toward the stern. The final tab hooks around one of the upright side supports. You may need to gently pull the deck back, to fit this tab. Squeeze the joint to neaten the seam.

Diagram B

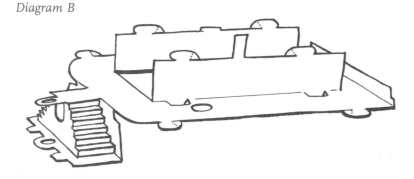

STEP 5: FIRST DECK

Fold the first (middle) deck (Part 3). See Diagram B. Take your time. The staircase is quite easy if you study the diagram and fold the part carefully in stages, finally squashing the assembly inward to ensure that the creases are really sharp. Now fix the deck. First insert the tabs that hold the staircase in place, then fold and insert tabs that hold the deck in place on the yellow side walls of the lower deck. These tabs and their corresponding slots are marked with blue spots. Finally, fold and insert the four outer tabs in their slots in the sides.

STEP 6: PROMENADE DECK

Fold the promenade (top) deck (Part 4). Study Diagram C and be especially careful with the stairways. Fold and insert the four inner tabs that fix the deck to the yellow inner walls of the deck below. Now fix the outer tabs, which hold the deck to the hull sides; starting with the center tabs. These pull through a gap in the handrail. See Diagram C. Finally, fix the end tabs on each side, and the two tabs that fix the stern.

STEP 7: WHEELHOUSE, ROOF

Fold the wheelhouse (Part 5) and the roof (Part 6). The wheelhouse roof decorations pass through the slots in the wheelhouse roof, and then the wheelhouse is fixed to the top deck (make sure it's the right way around!), and the tabs may be gently pulled through from below. The American flag (Part 7) may now also be fixed; pull through the W-shaped slot on the top deck (see Diagram C). Now fix the roof and wheelhouse assembly to the top deck. Start with the middle tabs (the red and green navigation lights). The front part of the roof folds down in two steps, two small tabs fix the lower section, then the front part (colored yellow, with a double door and two windows) passes through the gap in the upper deck and forms a front wall below. The rear end of the top deck is secured by two locking tabs, and the two stovepipes pass through the slots at the back of the roof. Finally, the end is tucked into the gap between the deck and deckhouse top. Study Diagram C to see the general arrangement.

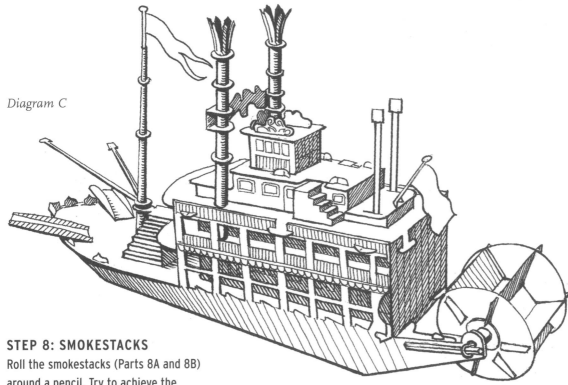

Diagram C

STEP 8: SMOKESTACKS

Roll the smokestacks (Parts 8A and 8B) around a pencil. Try to achieve the thinnest diameter you can. Take the six black rings (Parts 9), and the decorative center strut (Part 10). Fold the center strut as indicated (note that the fold lines are indicated by white dotted lines on this part). Thread two rings onto each chimney, and push up toward the top of the chimney as shown on Diagram C. Now join the two chimneys by threading on the center strut. Finally, thread on the two remaining rings. Now that the assembly is complete, insert the chimneys into their holes on the top deck. It helps to turn the chimneys as you push them in, threading through the holes on the middle deck, to project them about one-quarter inch below the deck. Finally, adjust for best effect and fold out the decorative spikes at the top of each stack.

STEP 9: FRONT MAST

Carefully curve the mast (Part 11) by rolling around a pencil. You will need to get it quite small, so roll the tube across a flat surface until it is small enough for the rings to fit around, bearing in mind that the top is the narrower end. Now thread the two spars (Parts 12A and 12B) onto the mast to about two inches from the bottom. Next, thread on the brown rings (Parts 13A and 13B), approximately equal distances apart to hold the mast together. Finally, insert the mast into the upper support bracket (this is the hole at the top of the staircase on the front deck), then through the hole in the deck, down to the bottom of the hull. Finally, adjust the position of the spars for best appearance.

STEP 10: GANGPLANKS

Fold the two gangplanks (Parts 14A and 14B). Insert into the slots in the front deck. The spars on the mast were used to raise and lower the gangplanks (like a crane), so they should be adjusted to be directly above the gangplanks.

STEP 11: FLAG

Fold the yellow flag (Part 15). Insert into the top of the mast.

STEP 12: PADDLE ASSEMBLY

Fold the paddle (Part 16). Both ends should meet, with the colored side out. Fold each of the paddle ends (Parts 17A and 17B) into a star shape (see Diagram D, which shows an end view of this part). You will find a small green spot on the INSIDE of one of the paddle ends. These two parts should be joined. Push the two tabs of one of the folded paddle blades into the paddle end, and repeat, working your way around the wheel until the two ends are inserted holding the assembly together. The sequence for inserting and locking each pair of paddle blades is shown in Diagram E. When you have finished, repeat for the other end. Next, cut and roll the paddle axle (Part 18). Insert the end with the green spot into the paddle assembly. It helps to roll the axle extra tight and twist gently as you insert it into the paddle. Make sure the axle isn't twisted. When the axle is assembled push on the washers (Parts 19A and 19B).

Diagram D

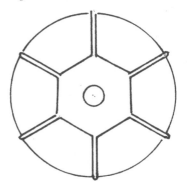

STEP 13: FINISHING PADDLE

You will now need two rubber bands. It's important to use the right size. They should be about three inches long, a little shorter than the paddle axle, and made from thin rubber (not the thick, flat type of rubber band). To fit the bands, first make a loop of thin wire or string, and thread it through the axle to pull the bands through. Hook one end over the tabs at the end of the axle with the green dot on it. Next, poke the other end of the bands through the small holes on the paddle support. Thread the black washers with

small holes (Parts 20A and 20B) over the ends of the rubber bands sticking out from the paddle assembly and secure in place with a wooden matchstick on either side (see Diagram C).

STEP 14: ADJUSTING PADDLE

Now thread the other end of the paddle axle through the large hole in the right-hand paddle support. Check that the paddle is able to turn freely. If it touches the support, adjust it by sliding the paddle on its axle. Now wind the paddle up. About thirty turns of the wheel should give a good run, but you will need to experiment. A drop of cooking oil applied to the wheel bearing may improve the running. Note that the wheel will whiz around freely outside the water, but in the water it will run slowly and for quite a while.

Diagram E

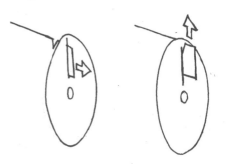

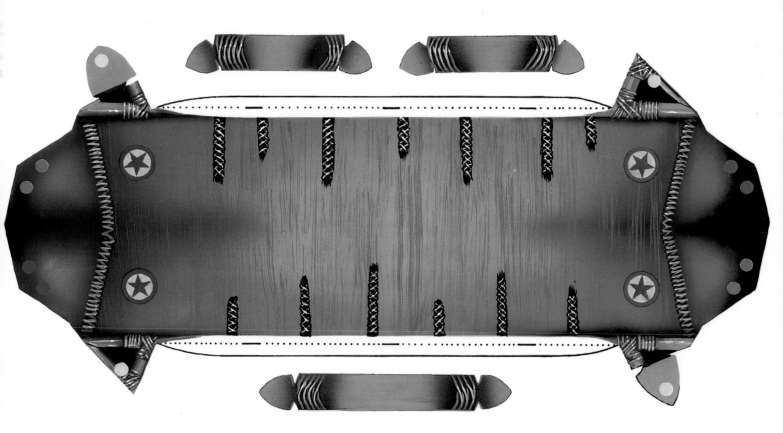

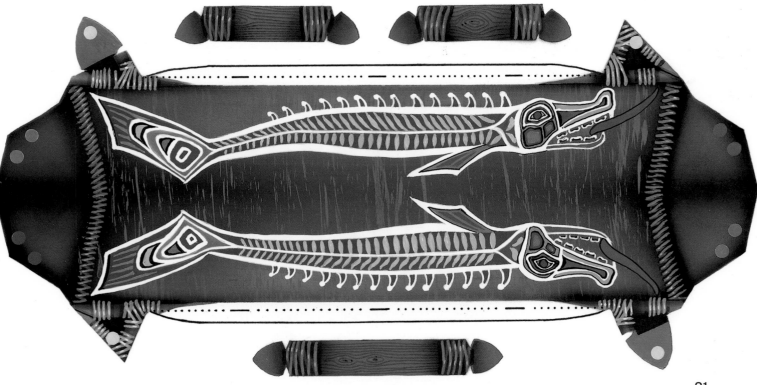

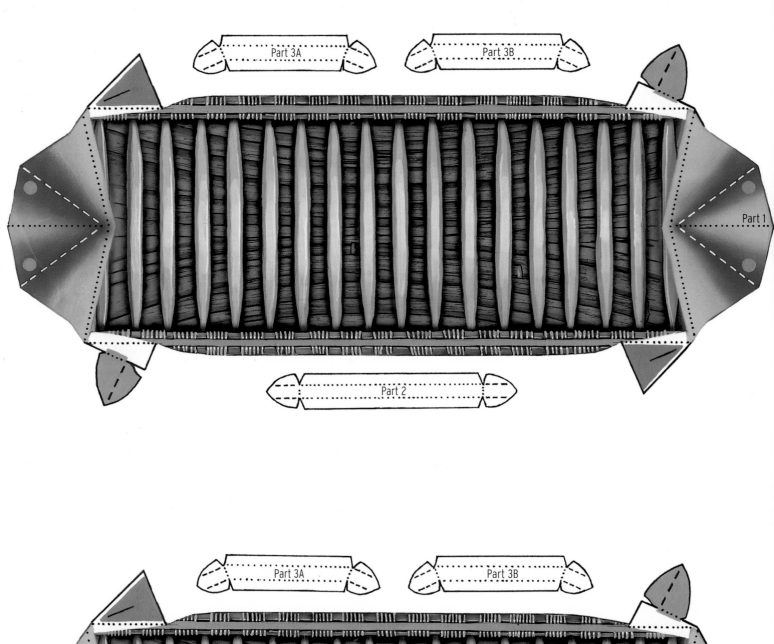

Part 3A

Part 3B

Part 1

Part 2

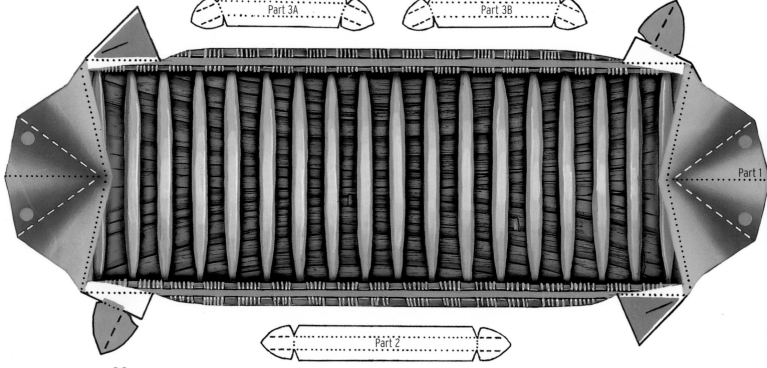

Part 3A

Part 3B

Part 1

Part 2

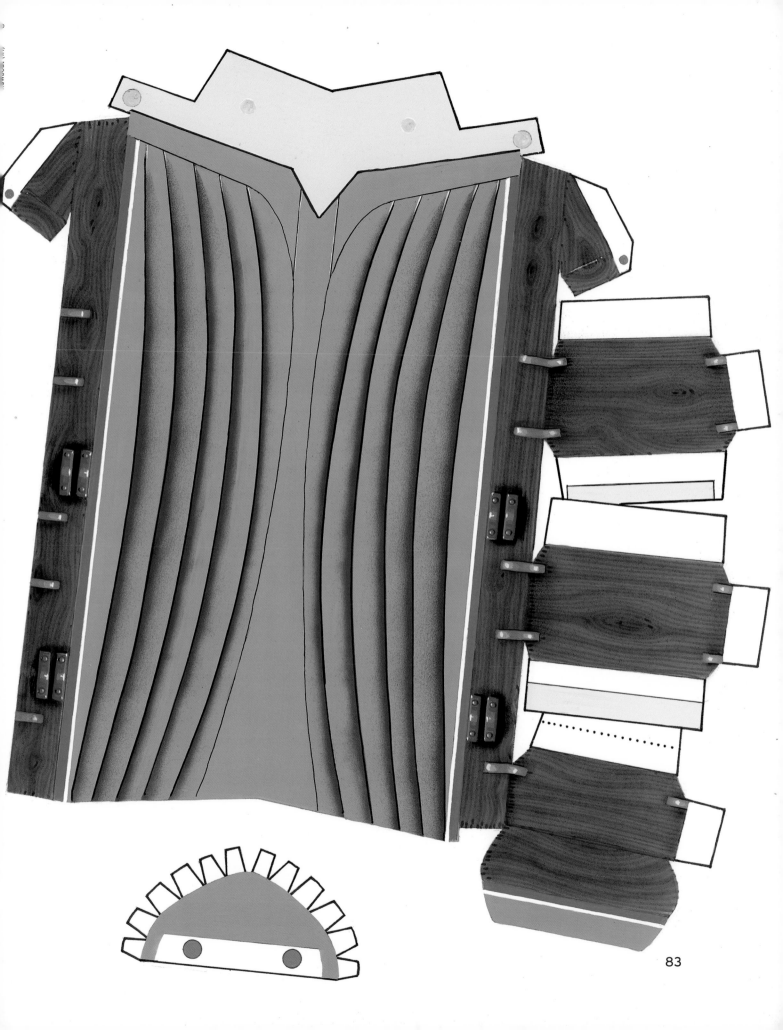

Part 1

Part 2

84

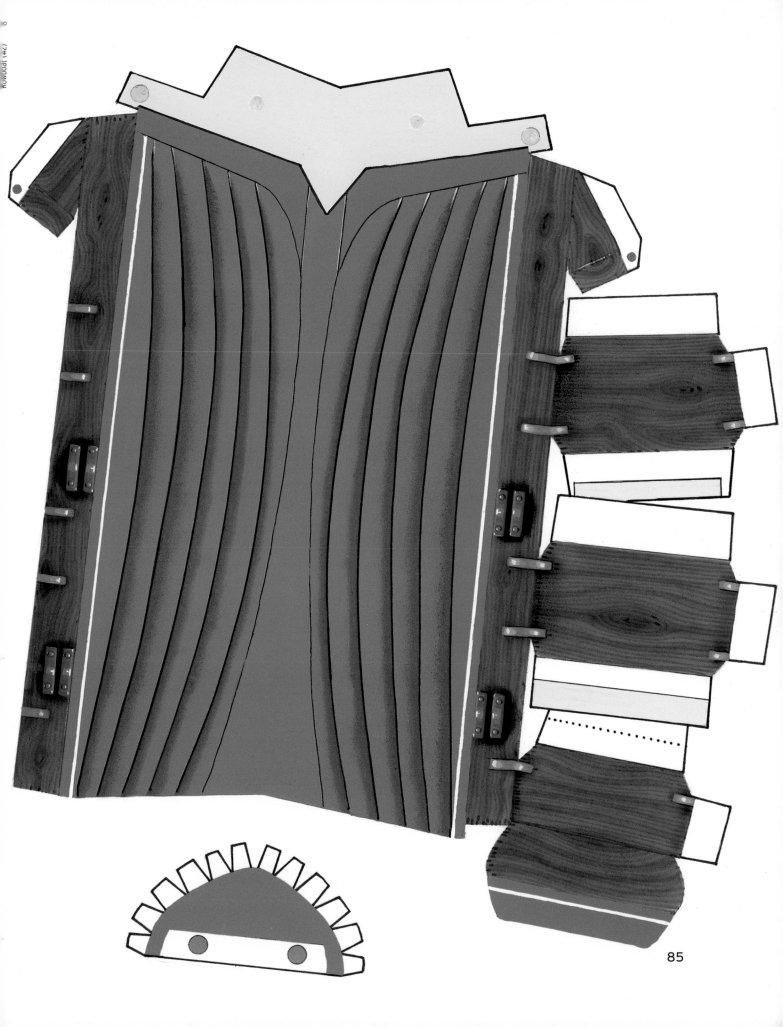

Part 1

Part 2

86

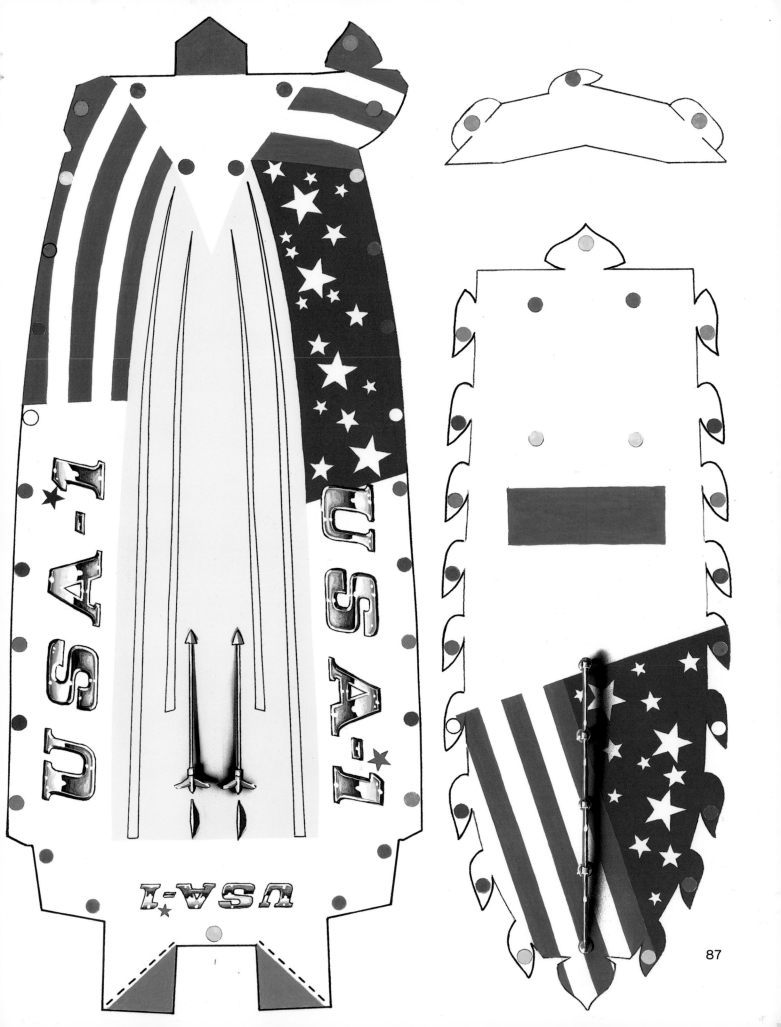

87

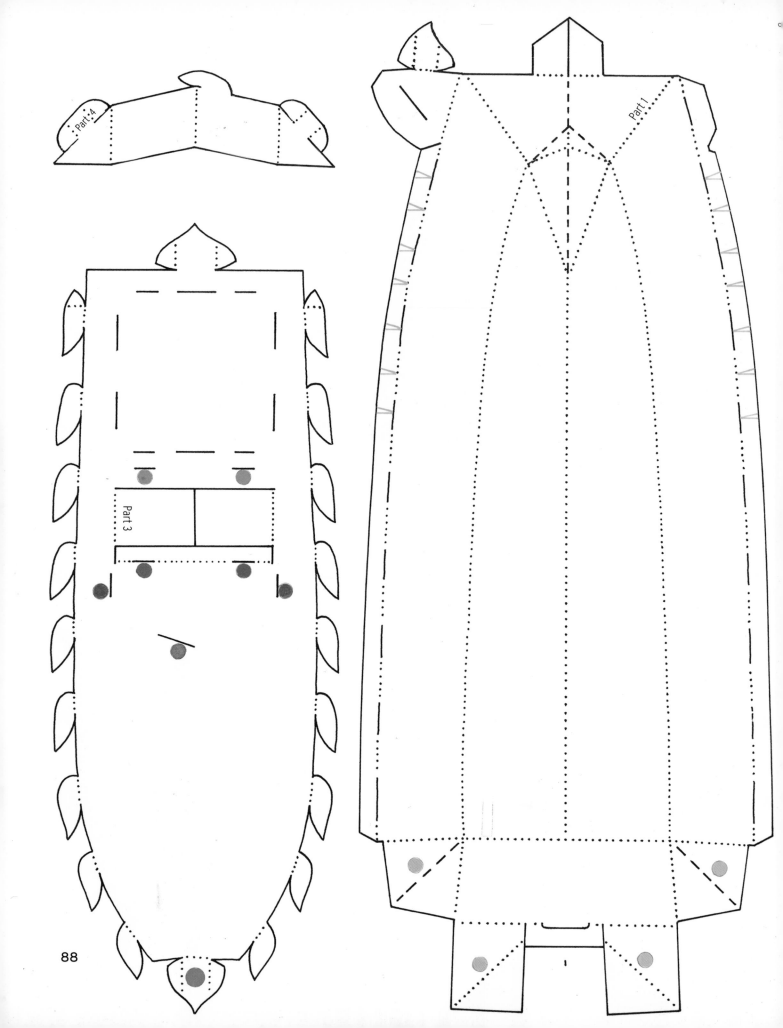

Part 4

Part 3

Part 1

88

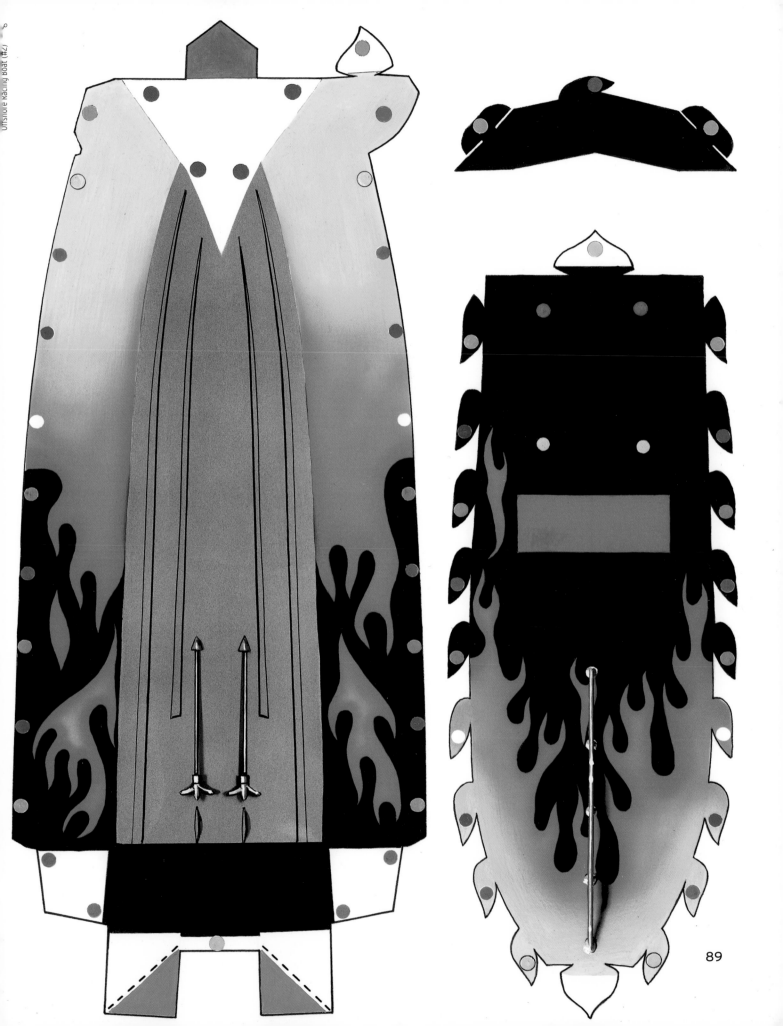

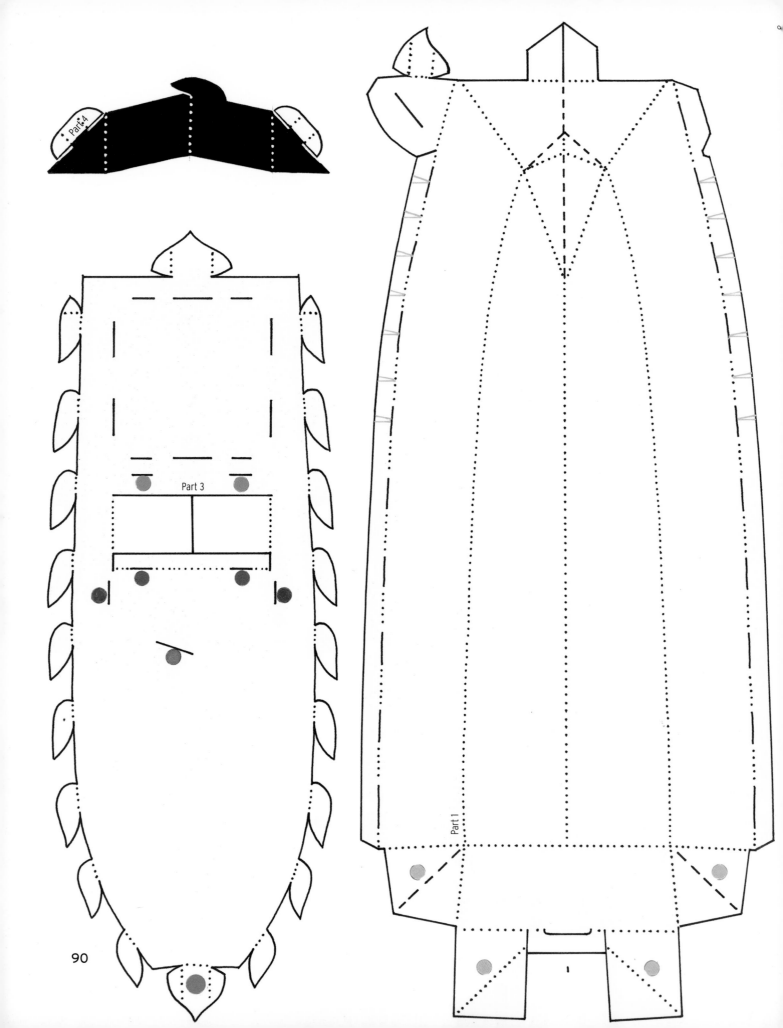

Part 4

Part 3

Part 1

90

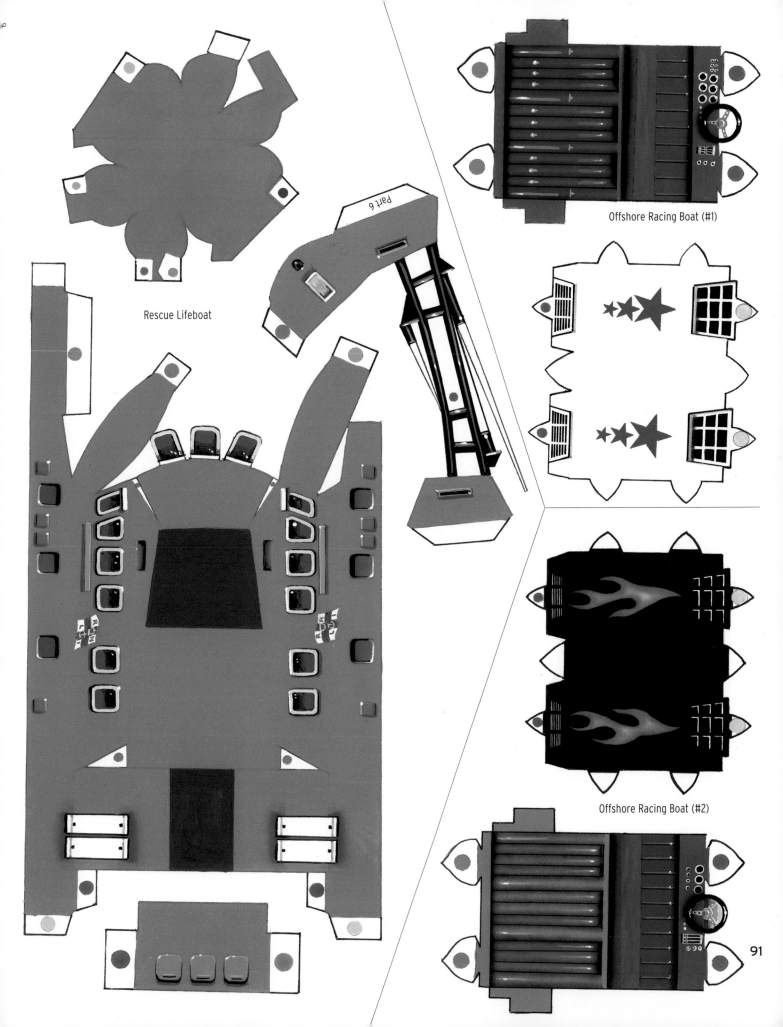

Rescue Lifeboat

Part 6

Offshore Racing Boat (#1)

Offshore Racing Boat (#2)

91

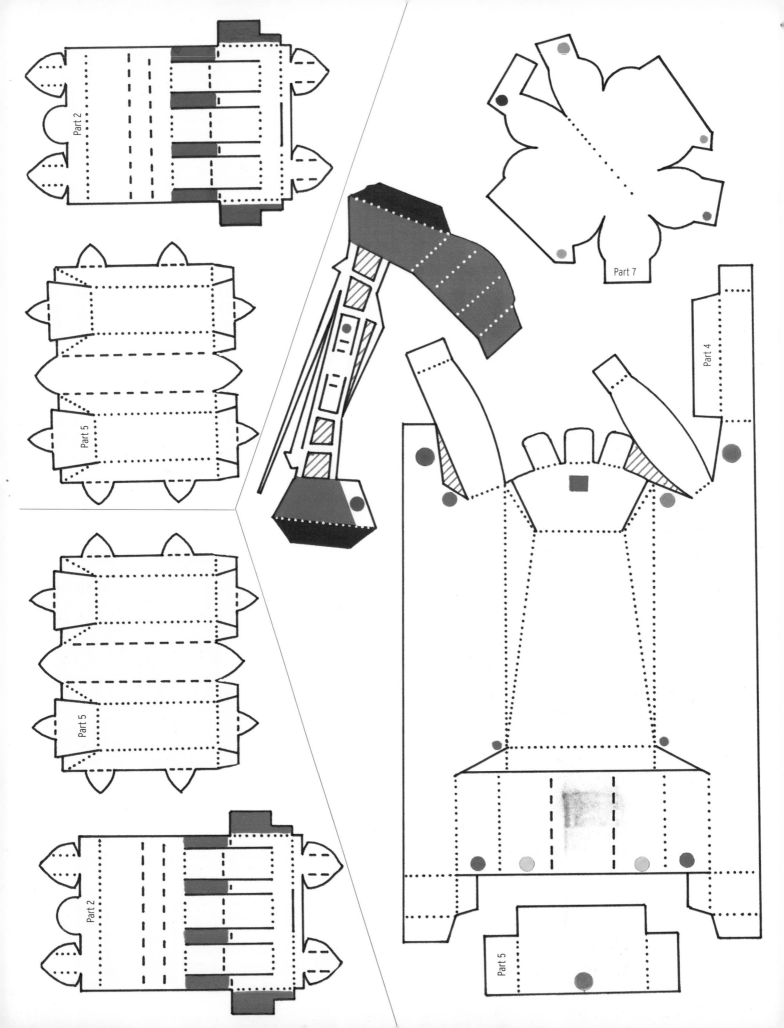

Part 2

Part 5

Part 5

Part 2

Part 7

Part 4

Part 5

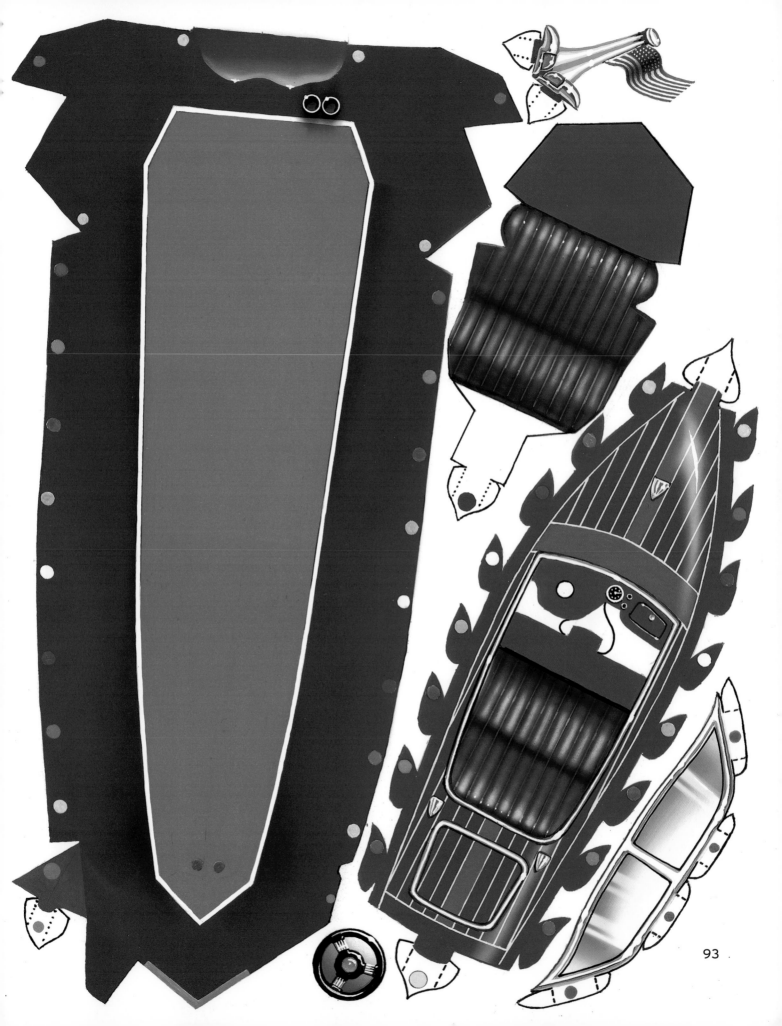

93

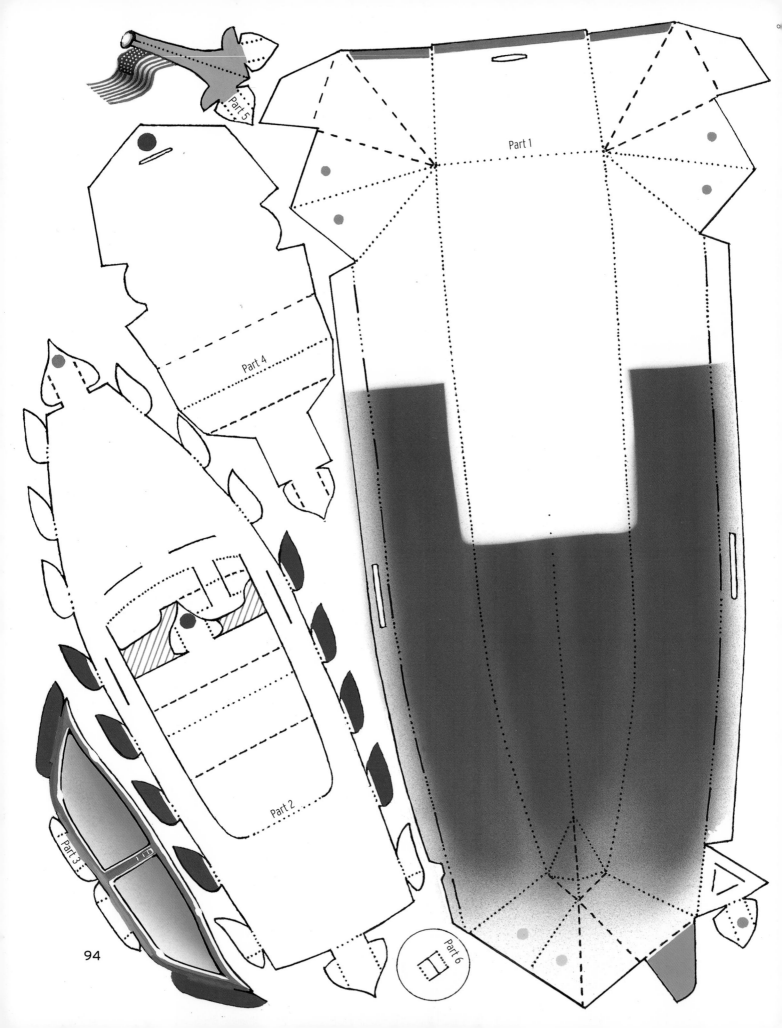

Part 5

Part 1

Part 4

Part 2

Part 3

Part 6

94

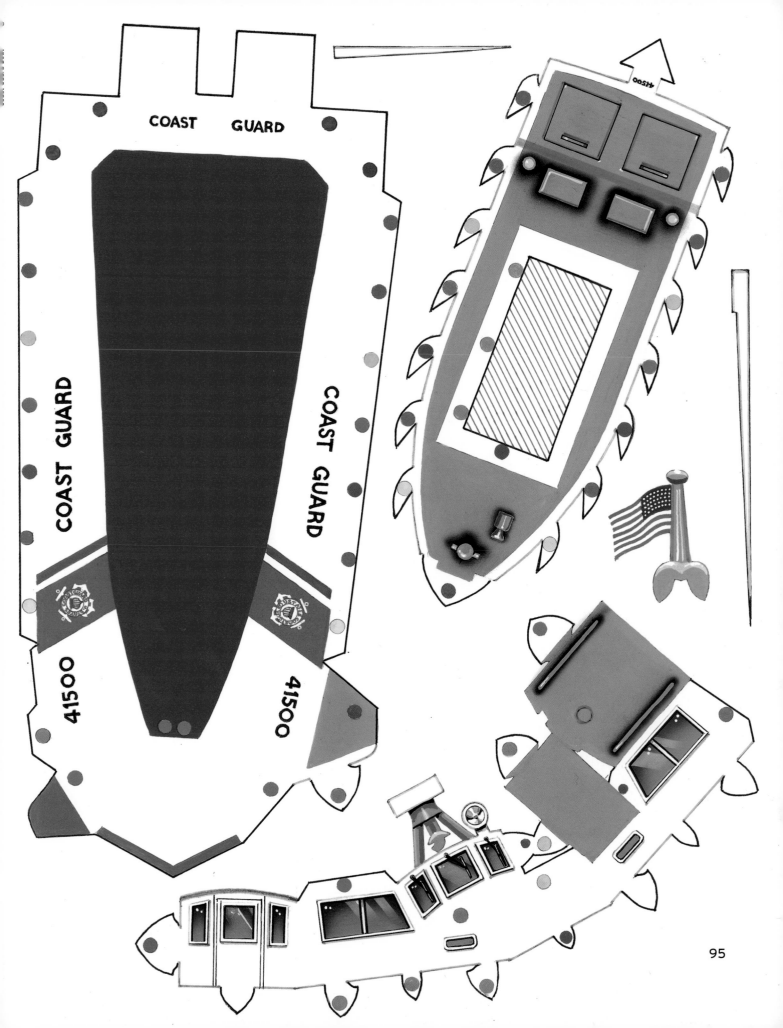

COAST   GUARD

COAST GUARD

COAST GUARD

41500

41500

41500

95

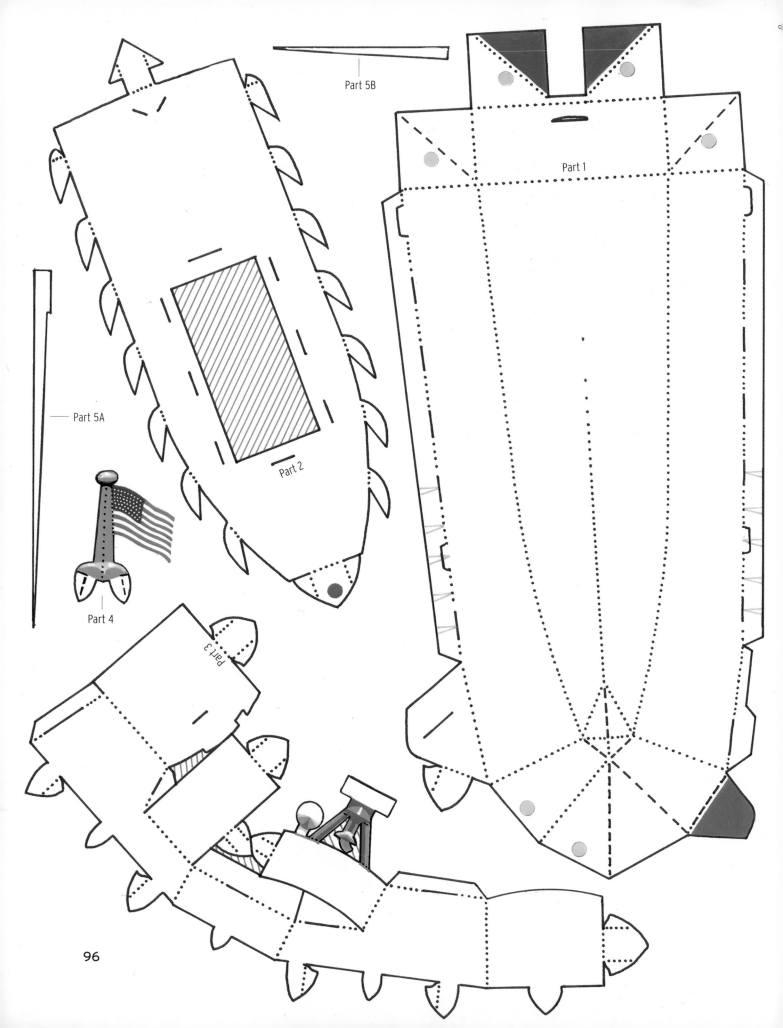

Part 5B

Part 1

Part 5A

Part 2

Part 4

Part 3

96

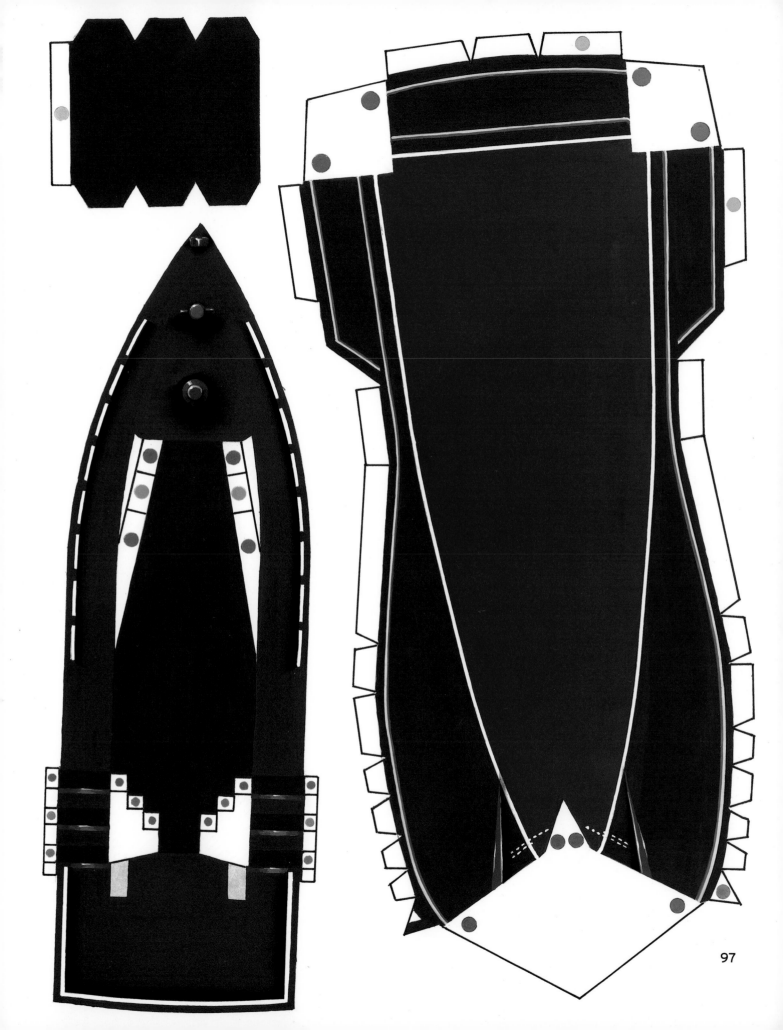

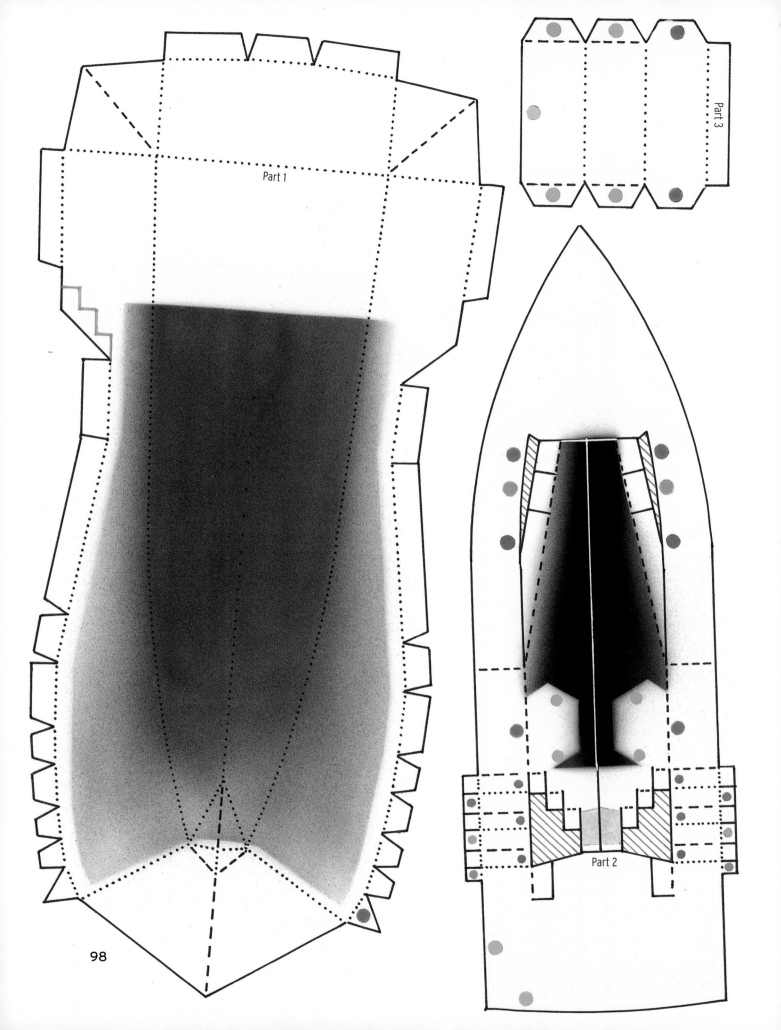

Part 1

Part 3

Part 2

98

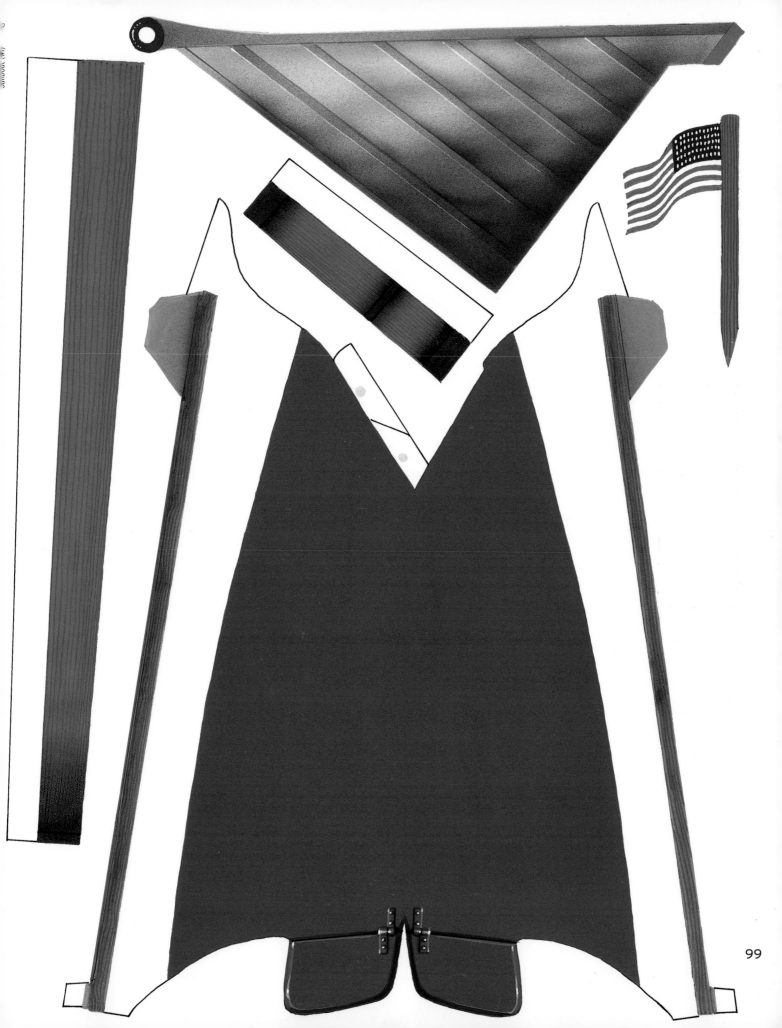

99

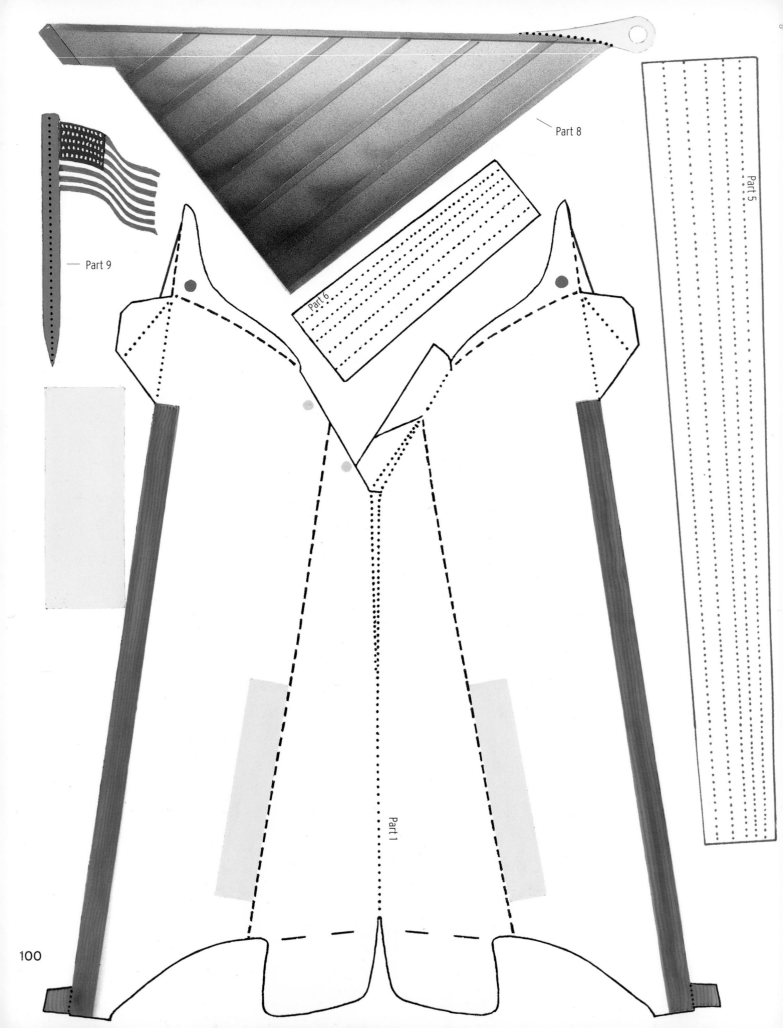

Part 8

Part 9

Part 5

Part 6

Part 1

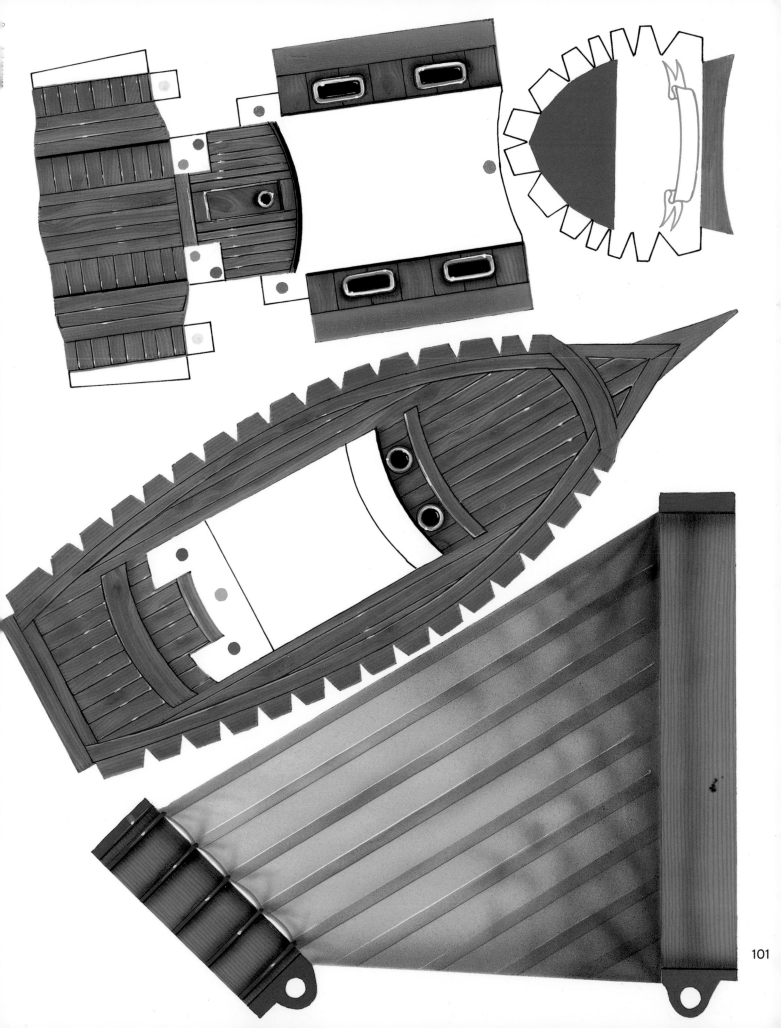

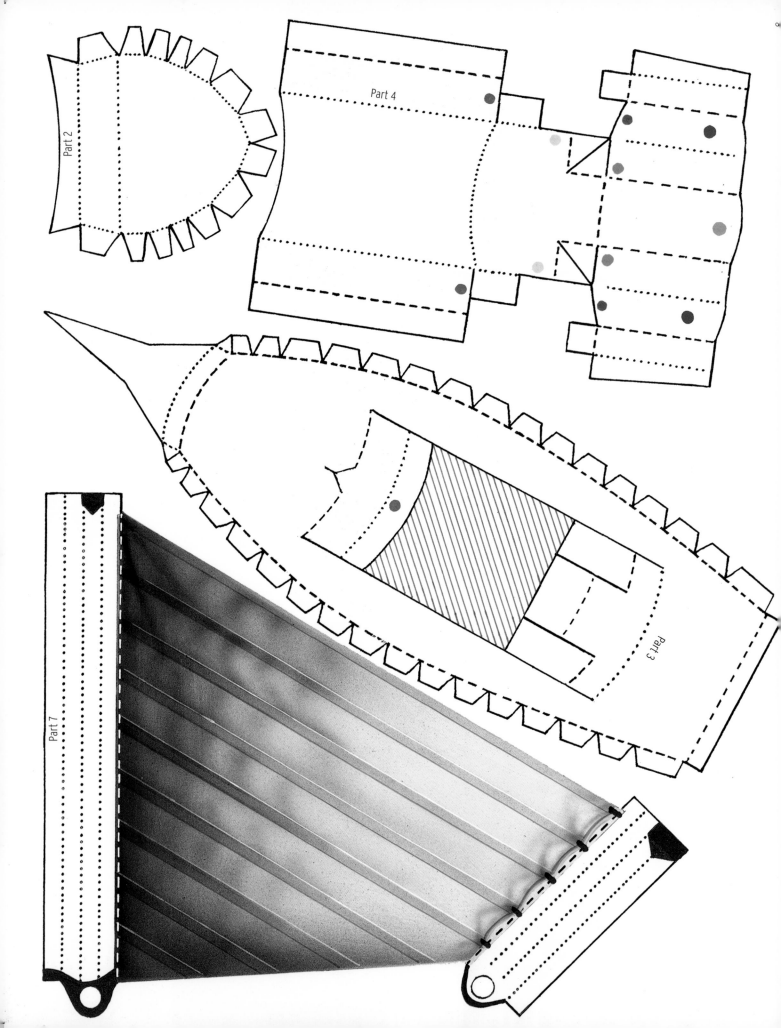

Part 2

Part 4

Part 3

Part 7

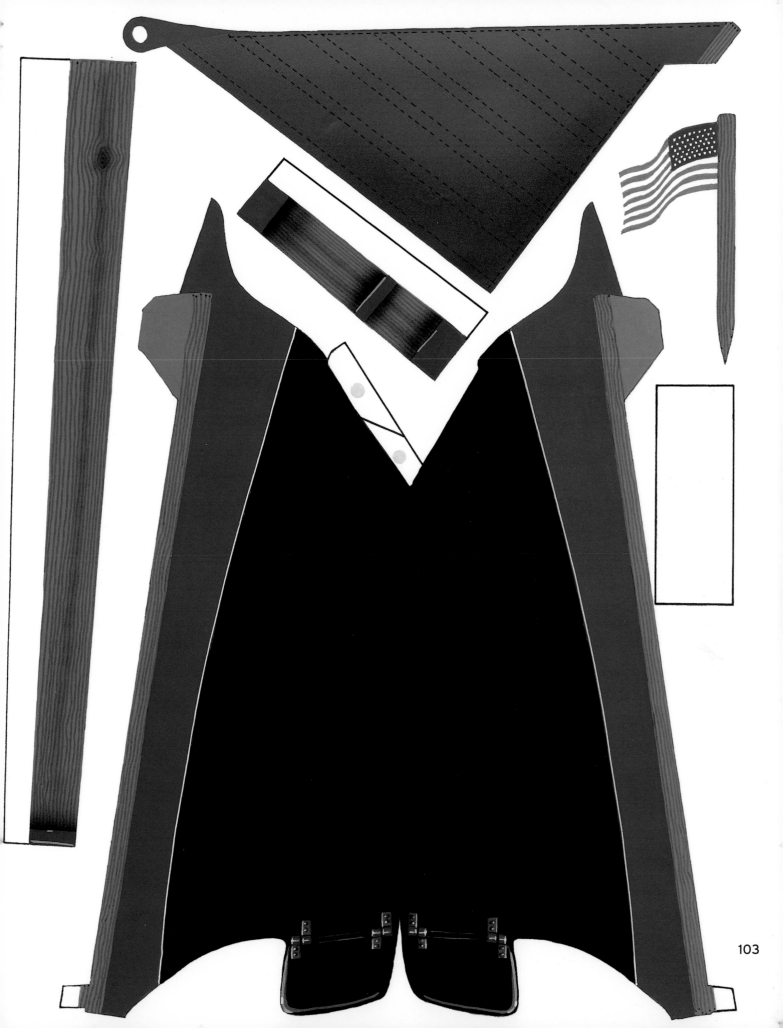

103

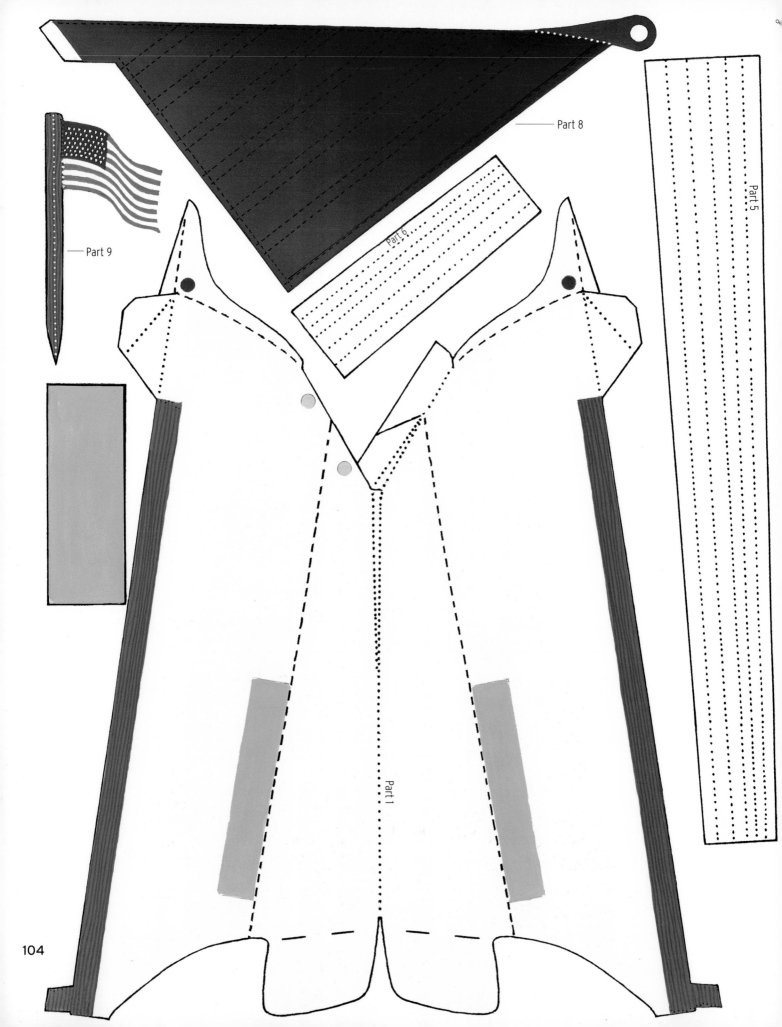

Part 8

Part 5

Part 9

Part 6

Part 1

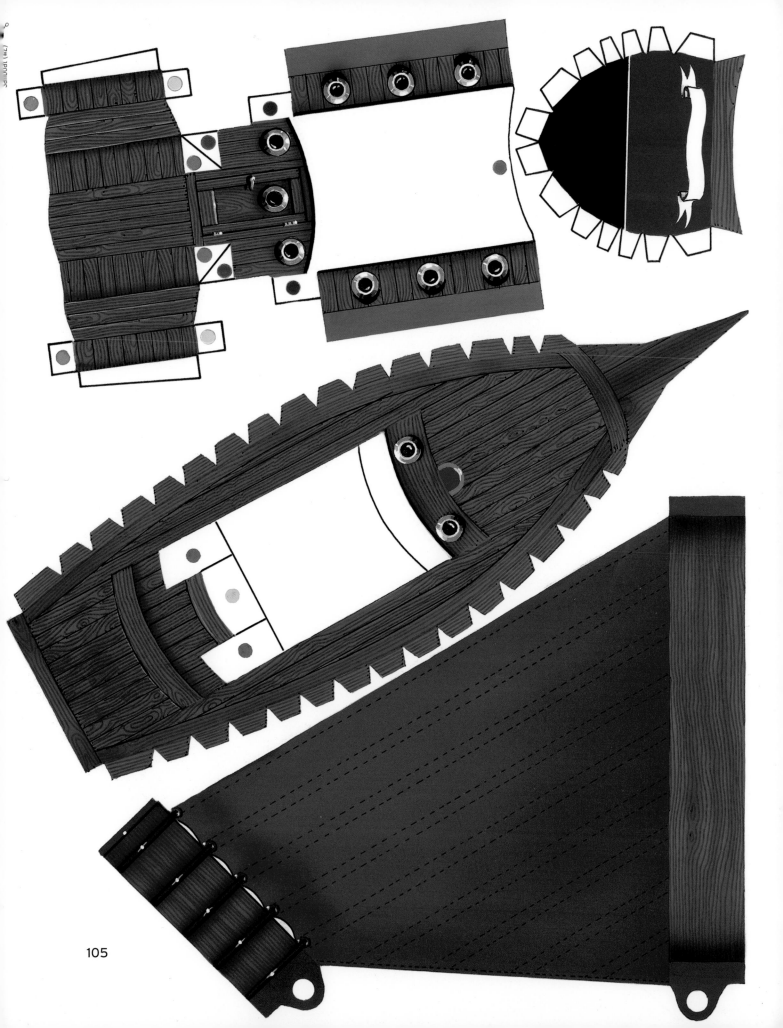

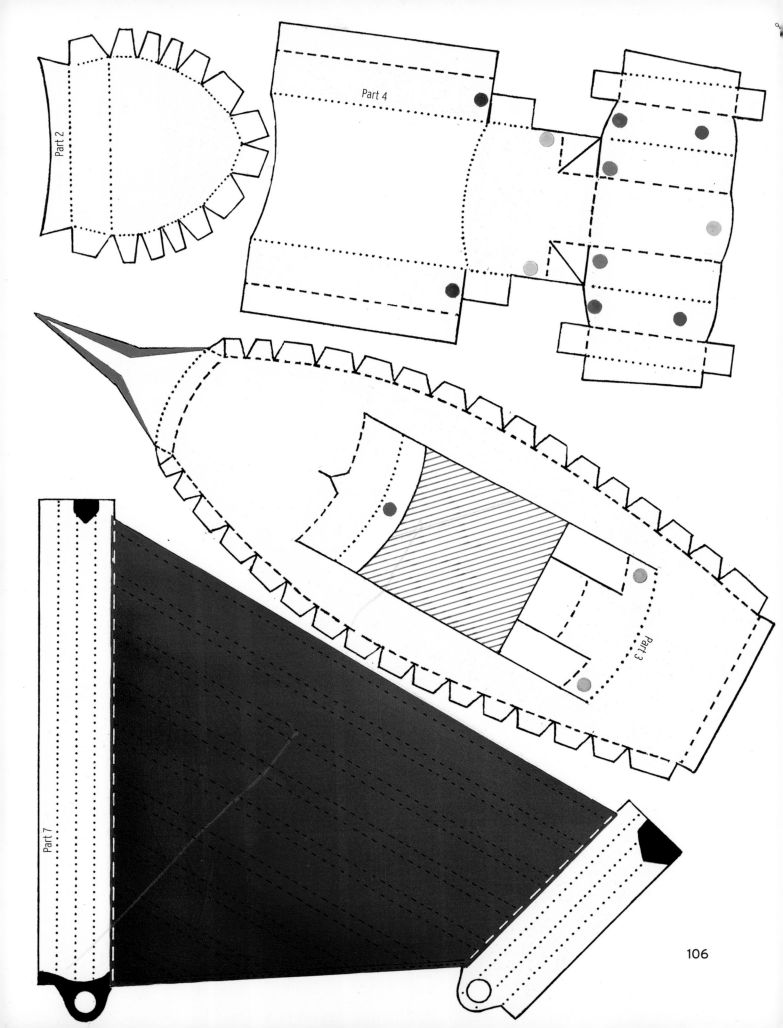

Part 2

Part 4

Part 3

Part 7

107

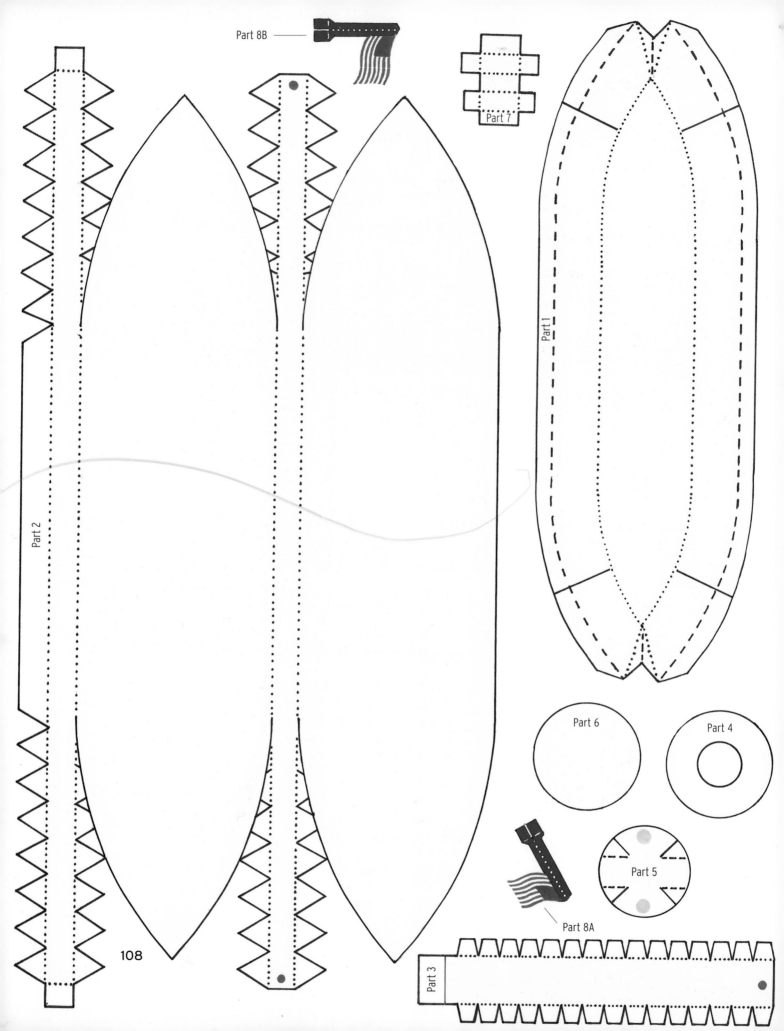

Part 8B

Part 7

Part 1

Part 2

Part 6

Part 4

Part 5

Part 8A

Part 3

108

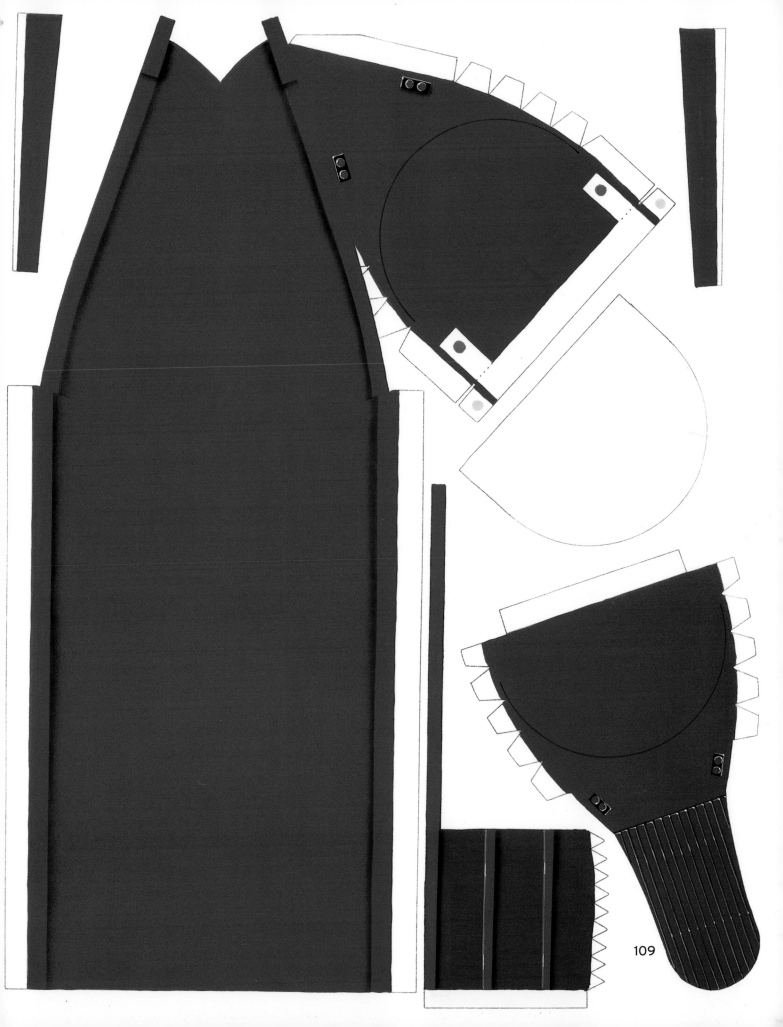

109

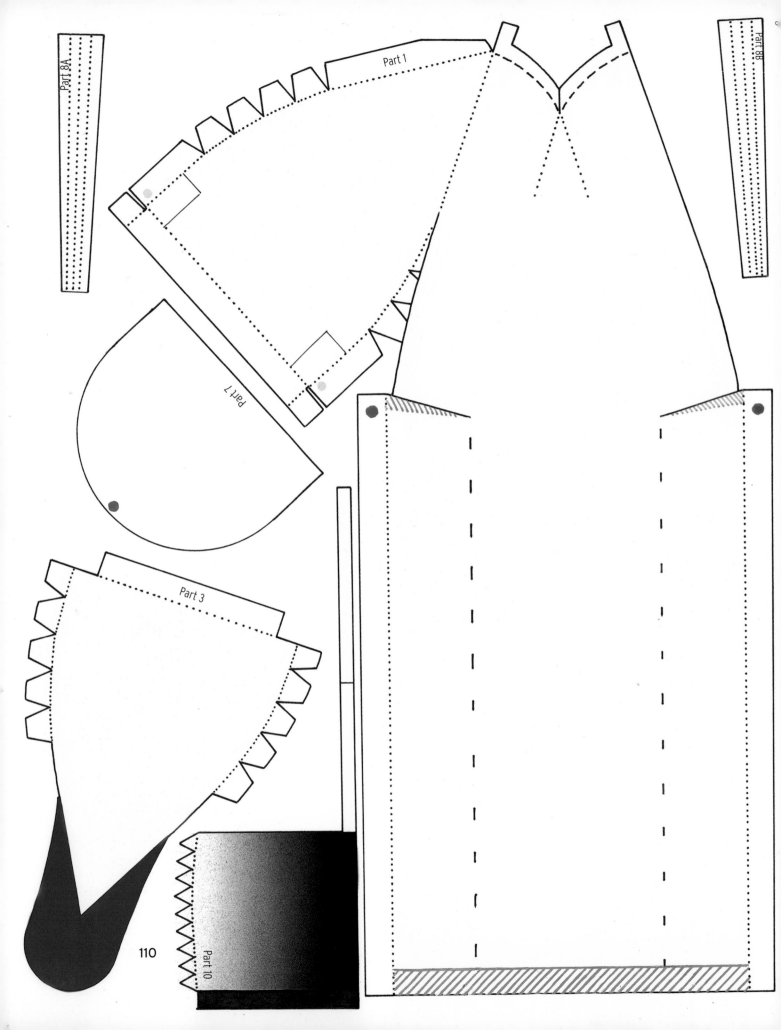

Part 8A

Part 8B

Part 1

Part 7

Part 3

110

Part 10

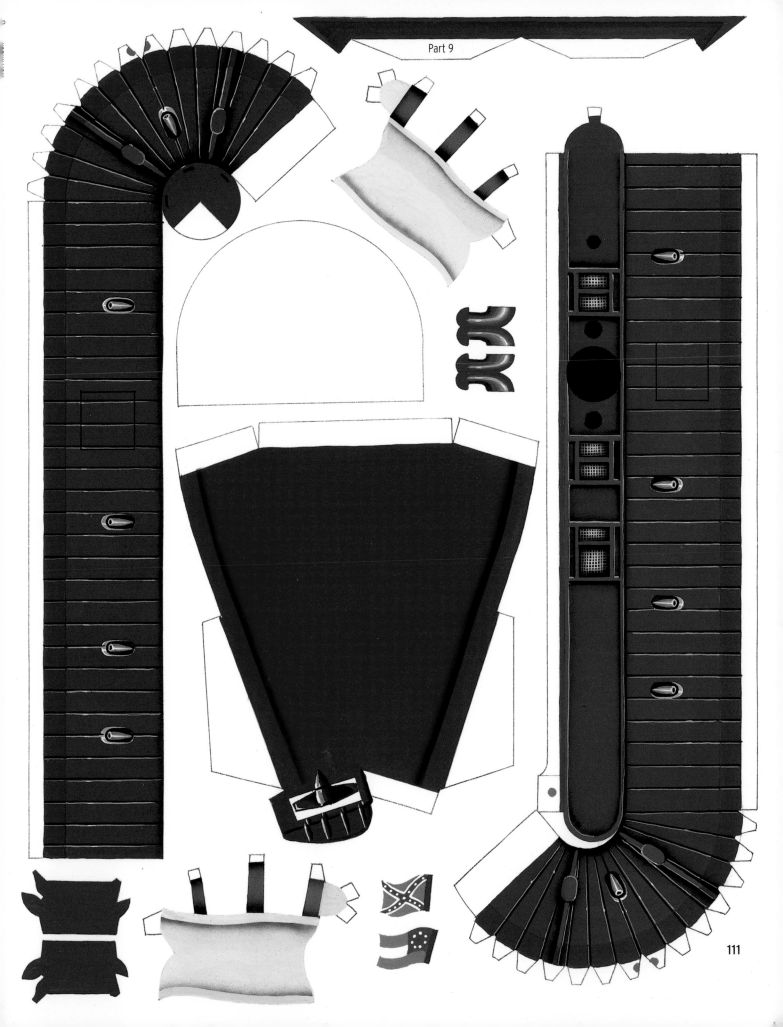

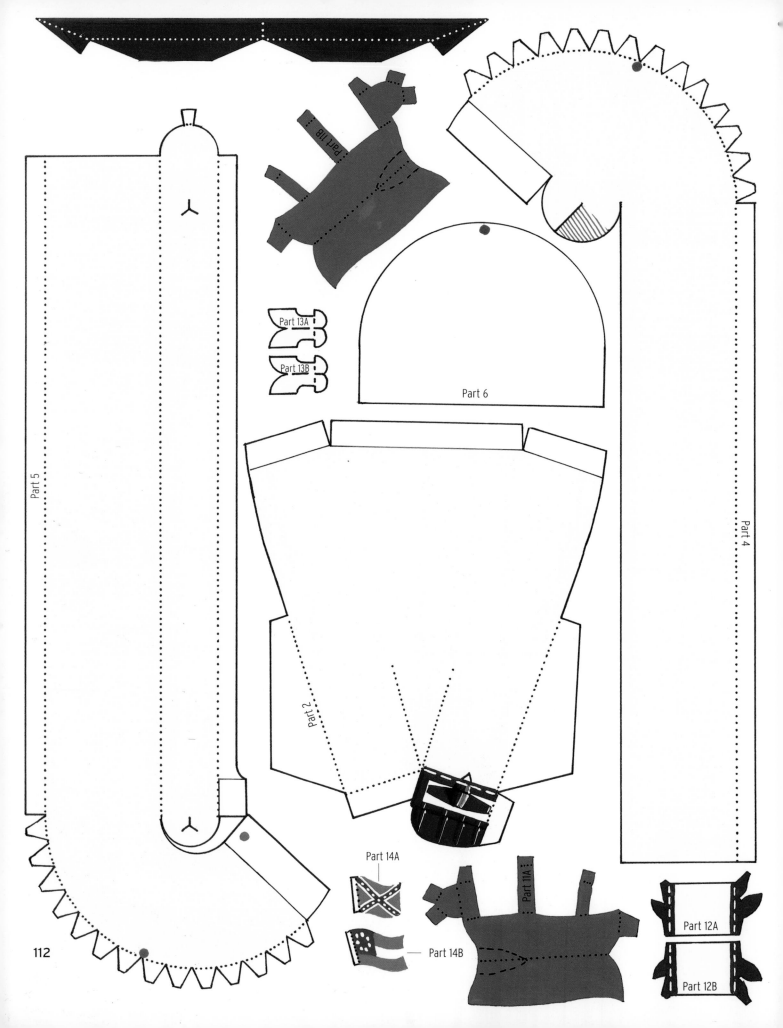

Part 9

Part 5

Part 13A

Part 13B

Part 6

Part 4

Part 2

Part 11B

Part 14A

Part 14B

Part 11A

Part 12A

Part 12B

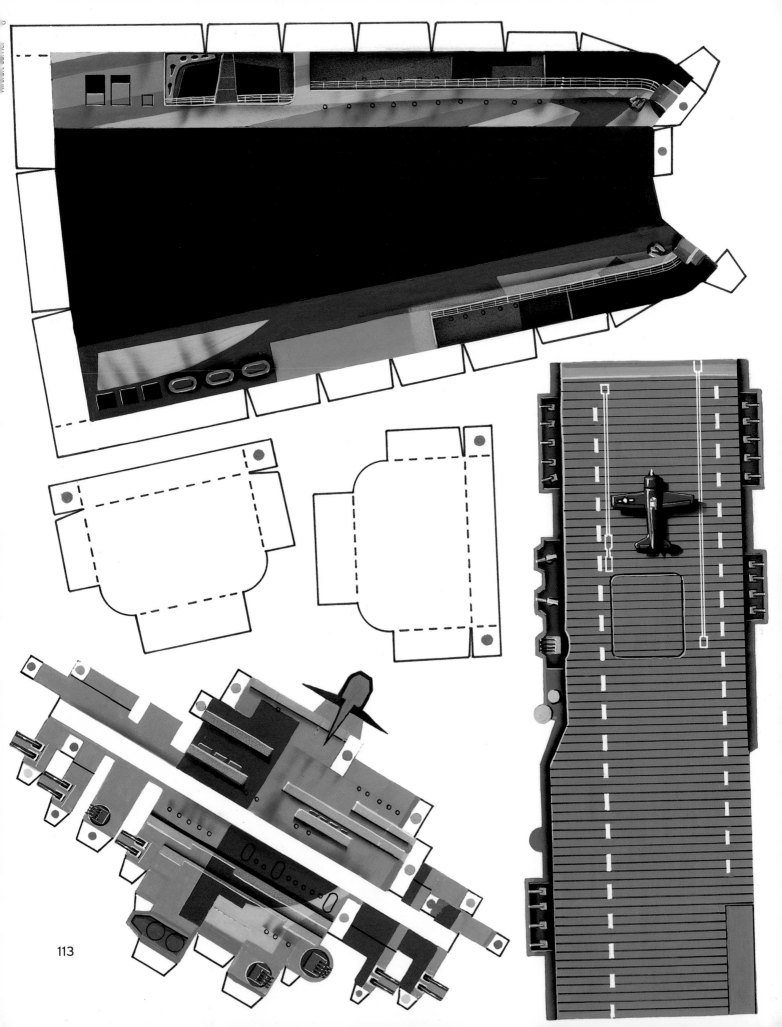

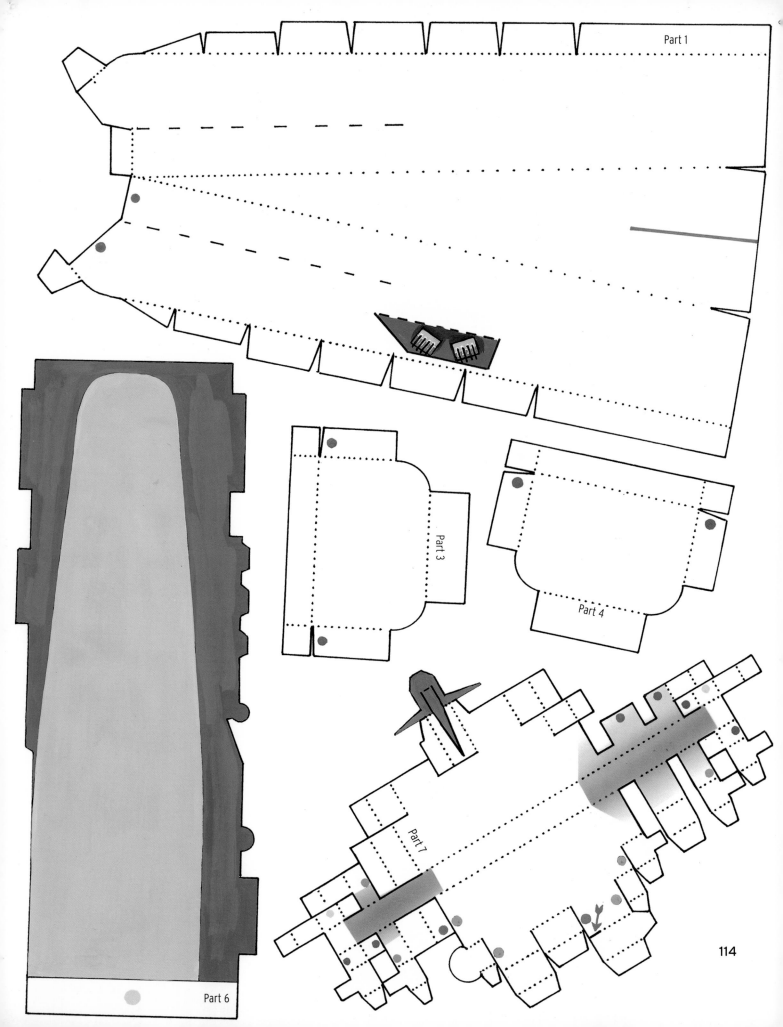

Part 1

Part 3

Part 4

Part 6

Part 7

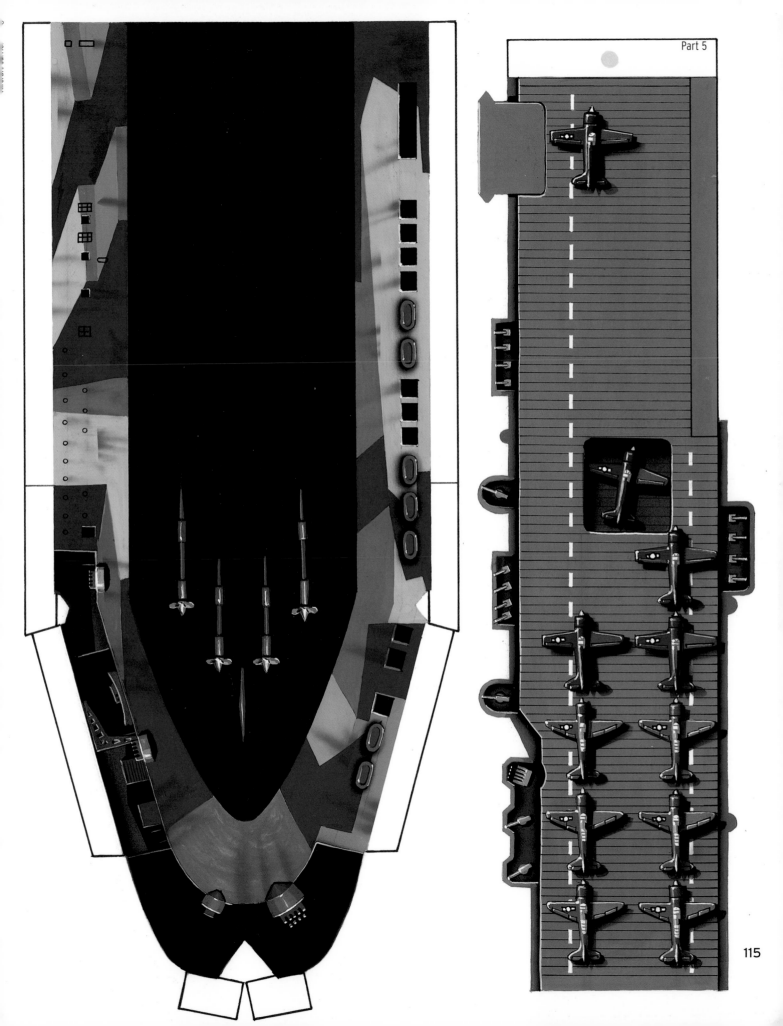

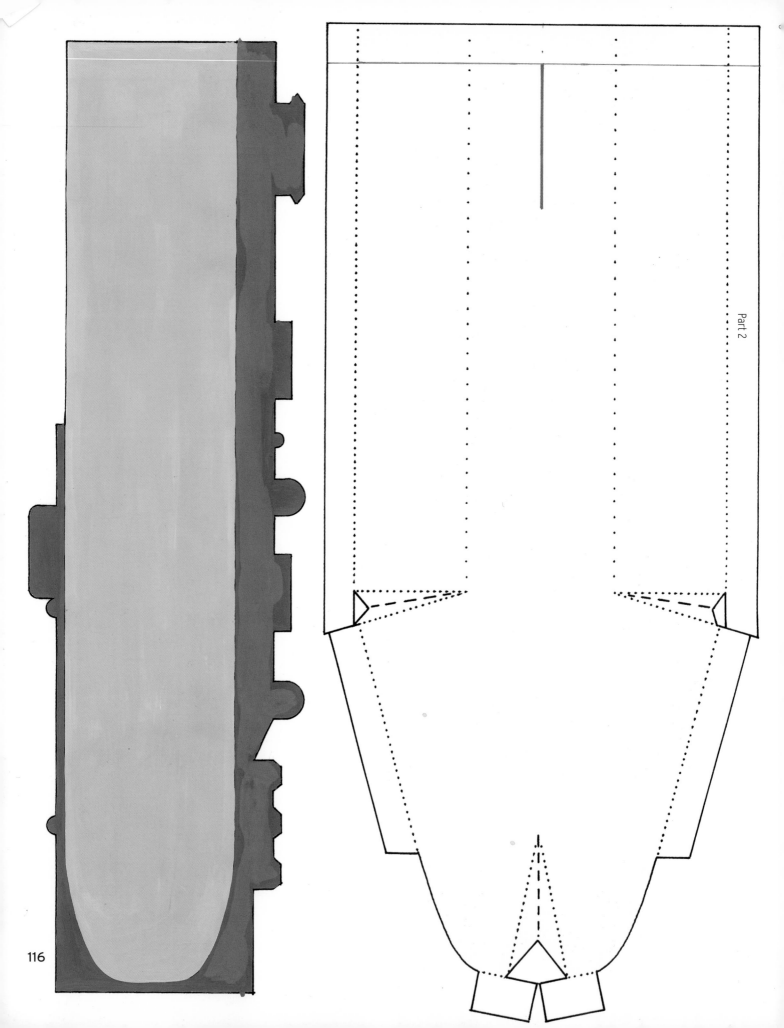

116

Part 2

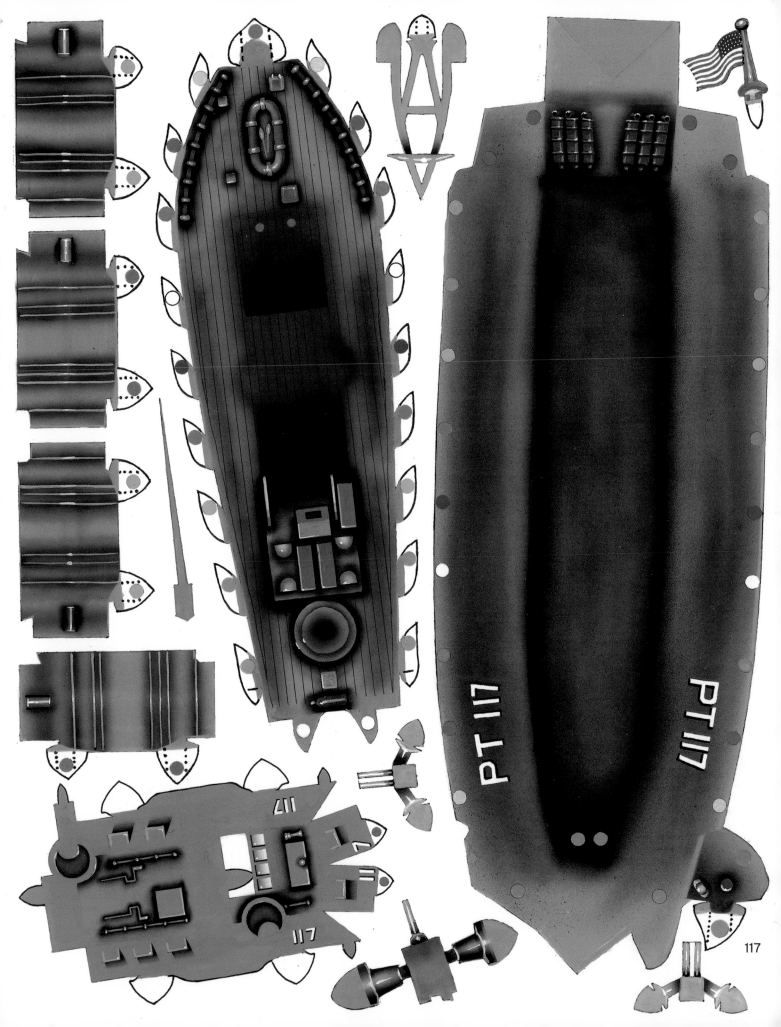

PT 117

PT 117

117

117

117

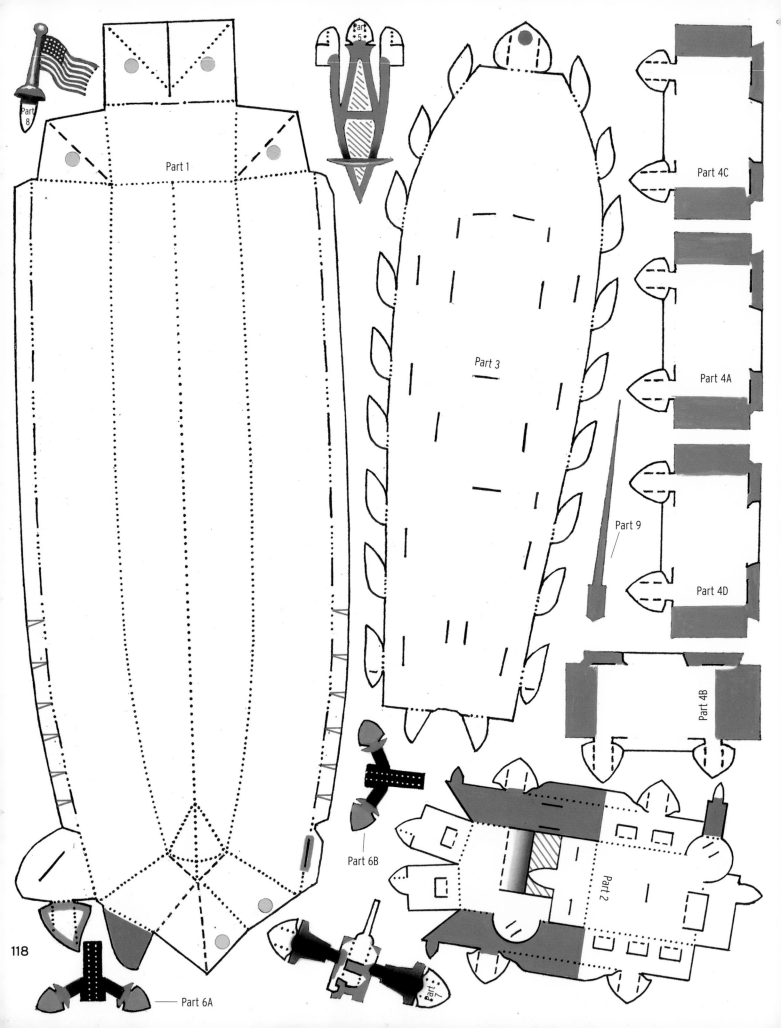

Part 8

Part 5

Part 1

Part 3

Part 4C

Part 4A

Part 9

Part 4D

Part 4B

Part 6B

Part 2

Part 6A

Part 7

118

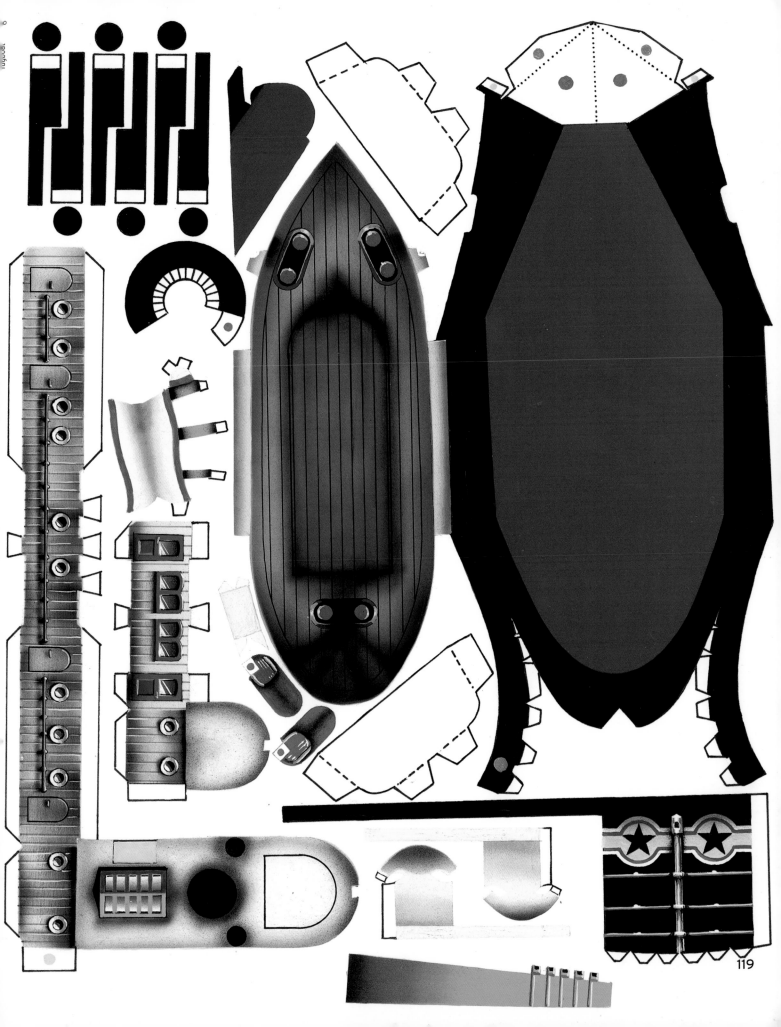

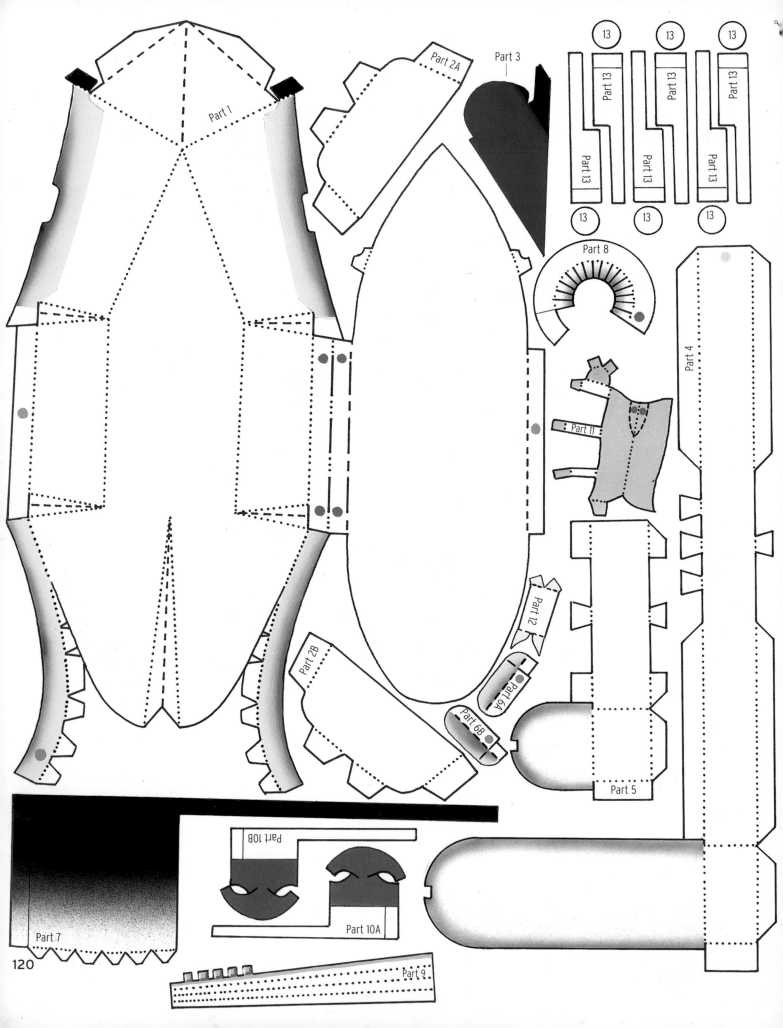

Part 1

Part 2A

Part 3

Part 13
Part 13
Part 13

Part 13
Part 13
Part 13

13 13 13

13 13 13

Part 8

Part 11

Part 4

Part 12

Part 2B

Part 6A

Part 6B

Part 5

Part 10B

Part 10A

Part 7

Part 9

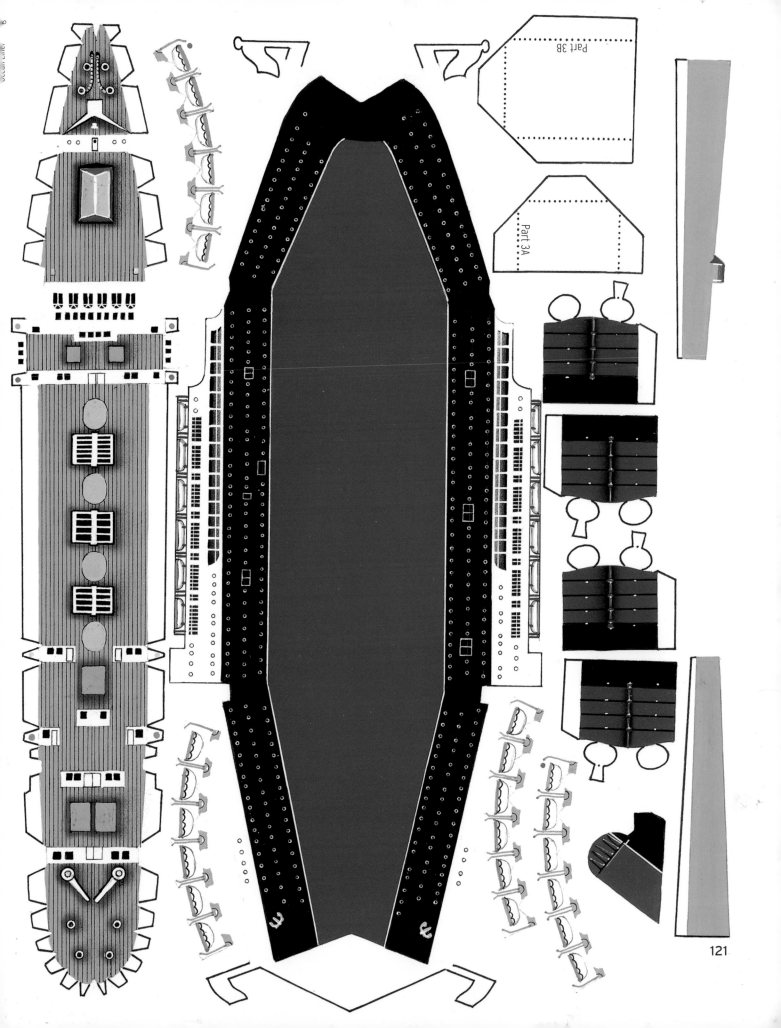

Part 3B

Part 3A

121

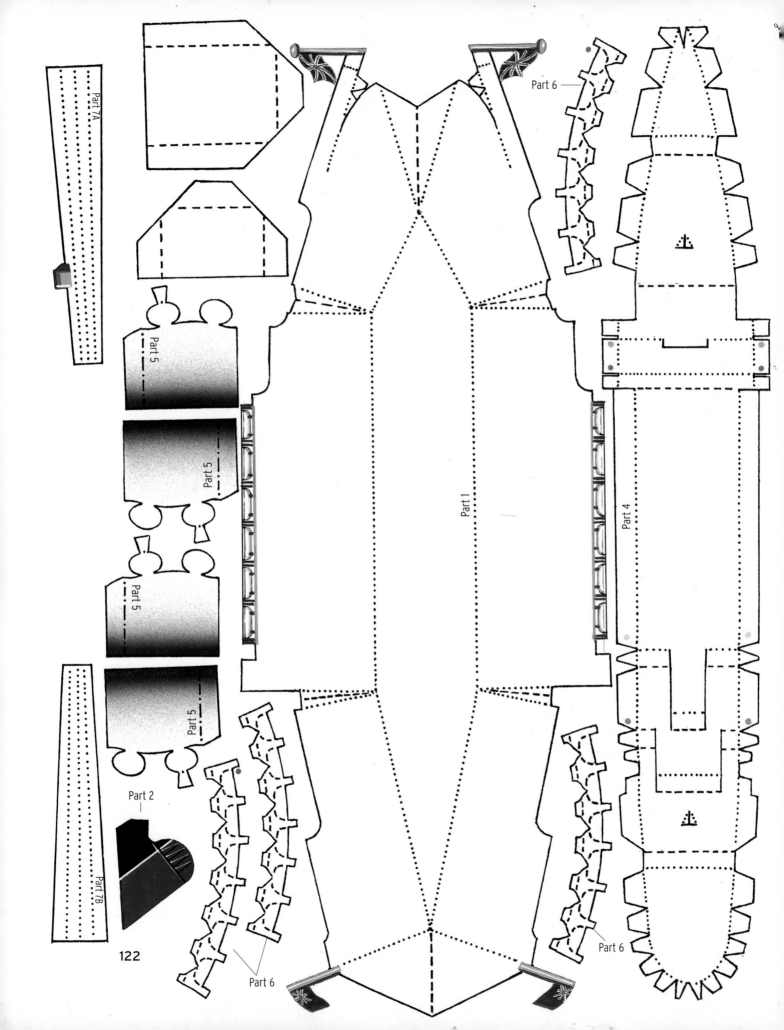

Part 7A

Part 6

Part 5

Part 5

Part 5

Part 1

Part 4

Part 6

Part 5

Part 2

Part 7B

122

Part 6

Part 6

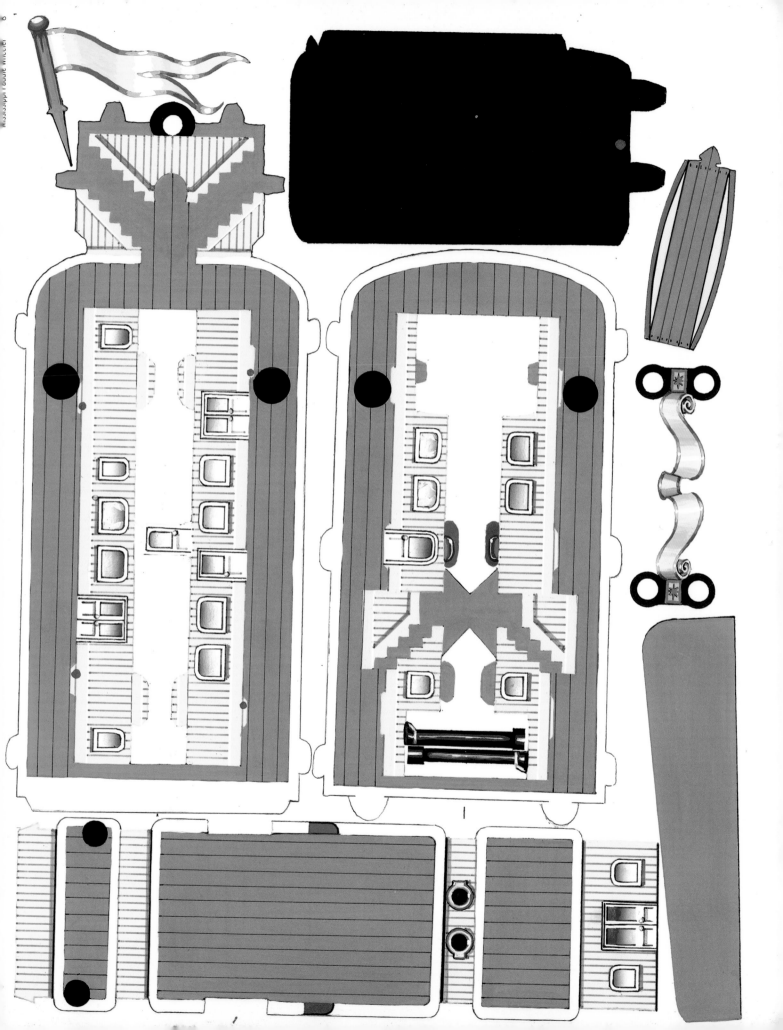

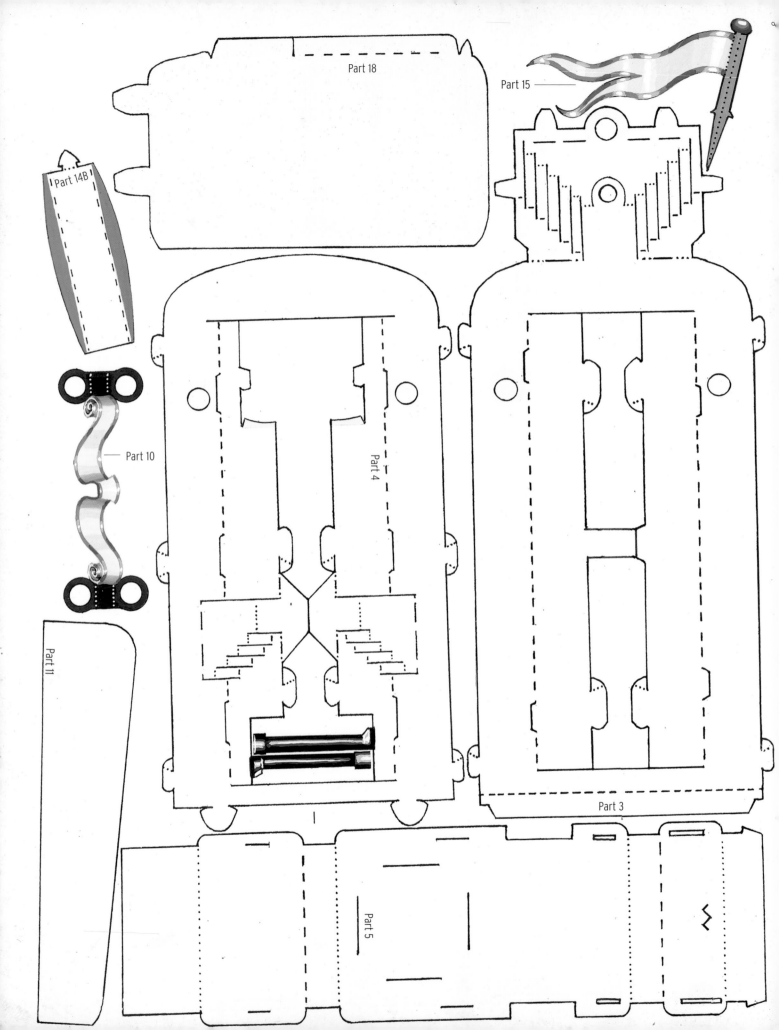

Part 18

Part 15

Part 14B

Part 10

Part 11

Part 4

Part 3

Part 5